100
PRAYERS

100
PRAYERS

INSPIRED BY THE
PSALMS

JULIE ACKERMAN LINK

Discovery House®
from Our Daily Bread Ministries

100 Prayers Inspired by the Psalms
© 2017 by Jay Link. All rights reserved.

Discovery House is affiliated with Our Daily Bread Ministries, Grand Rapids, Michigan.

Requests for permission to quote from this book should be directed to: Permissions Department, Discovery House, PO Box 3566, Grand Rapids, MI 49501, or contact us by email at permissionsdept@dhp.org.

All Scripture quotations, unless otherwise indicated, are taken from the Holy Bible, *New International Version*®, *NIV*®. Copyright © 1973, 1978, 1984, 2011 by Biblica, Inc.™ Used by permission of Zondervan. All rights reserved worldwide. zondervan.com. The "NIV" and "New International Version" are trademarks registered in the United States Patent and Trademark Office by Biblica, Inc.™

Scripture quotations marked TLB are taken from *The Living Bible*. Copyright © 1971 by Tyndale House Publishers, Inc., Wheaton, Illinois. All rights reserved.

Scripture quotations marked MSG are taken from *The Message*. Copyright © 1993, 1994, 1995, 1996, 2000, 2001, 2002. Used by permission of NavPress Publishing Group.

Scripture quotations marked NKJV are taken from the New King James Version. Copyright © 1982, by Thomas Nelson, Inc. Used by permission. All rights reserved.

Interior design by Beth Shagene

LIBRARY OF CONGRESS CATALOGING-IN-PUBLICATION DATA
Names: Link, Julie Ackerman, author.
Title: 100 prayers inspired by the Psalms / Julie Ackerman Link.
Other titles: One hundred prayers inspired by the Psalms
Description: Grand Rapids : Discovery House, 2017. | Includes index.
Identifiers: LCCN 2017016480 | ISBN 9781627077316 (pbk.)
Subjects: LCSH: Prayers. | Bible--Prayers.
Classification: LCC BS680.P64 L56 2017 | DDC 242/.722--dc23
LC record available at https://lccn.loc.gov/2017016480

Printed in the United States of America
Second printing in 2018

To George H. Ohman Jr.

A devoted husband, father, friend,
and follower of Jesus who consistently
and passionately modeled for Julie, me,
and countless others that worship
is more than a Sunday morning activity.
It is a personal identity manifested
in the everyday routines of one's life.
—Jay R. Link

CONTENTS

How It All Began

Any work of God begins with an inspiration. And any work of God comes with cost and sacrifice. But it is also true that any work of God truly takes shape and form when partnerships come together to make the inspiration a reality. This is the story behind this book.

It began when my wife Julie, a member of Calvary Church* in Grand Rapids, Michigan, united with worship pastor George Ohman Jr. around a common purpose: to lead the congregation of Calvary Church to worship God in spirit and in truth.

In the fall of 1998, the church was going through a season of rest, and the congregation was challenged to do less activity and to connect with God more. Julie used this opportunity to deepen her walk with the Lord by reading through the Bible in a year. She asked if I would join her, and I agreed. She developed a unique Bible-reading schedule that would have us read from the Old Testament and the New Testament each day. We both were in the habit of daily Bible reading, but we had never read the entire Bible in one year. It was an ambitious plan, but with mutual encouragement the prospect seemed doable.

Julie served on the worship committee of Calvary.

---

*Calvary Church was begun under the leadership of Dr. M. R. DeHaan, who also founded the parent organization of Discovery House, Our Daily Bread Ministries, in 1938.

At one of their monthly meetings, she shared what we were doing with George and said, "I wonder if this is something the entire congregation could embrace." George was intrigued with the idea but was not sure how it would work. Julie suggested, "What if we make the Sunday morning bulletin the tool to facilitate this? I will volunteer my time and take the lead, but we will need to work together." After careful thought, George responded, "Let's give it a try."

They agreed to revamp the entire bulletin, or worship folder as it's called at Calvary. Julie selected a Psalm related to the pastor's sermon, wrote a prayer that connected the Psalm to the first song sung by the congregation, and included the daily Bible readings. The worship folder became a way for the congregation to prepare for Sunday worship and to connect daily with God and his Word.

The idea worked. In fact, the readings worked so well that what was supposed to be Julie's private love gift to the congregation for a year continued for three years. Each week Julie spent countless hours working and reworking the worship folder—all the while collaborating with George to integrate the Psalms and her unique prayers into the flow and content of the service. Their collaboration became our little secret since her name was not mentioned on the bulletin. I remember watching as those seated around Julie and me in the morning service read her prayers in silent preparation for worship and then wondered aloud who had written them.

In April 2015, one of the last requests Julie had before she went to heaven was to see if I could have her prayers published so her sacrificial gift to our church could be made available to the church at large. I am delighted that Discovery House has agreed to compile her prayers and the related Psalms so her desire to see others deepen their relationship with Christ could be fulfilled.

JAY R. LINK

[1] O LORD, you have searched me
  and you know me.
[2] You know when I sit and when rise;
  you perceive my thoughts from afar.

[5] You hem me in—behind and before;
  you have laid your hand upon me.
[6] Such knowledge is too wonderful for me,
  too lofty for me to attain.

[14] I praise you because I am fearfully and
    wonderfully made;
  your works are wonderful,
  I know that full well.

[17] How precious to me are your thoughts, O God!
  How vast is the sum of them!

[23] Search me, O God, and know my heart;
  test me and know my anxious thoughts.
[24] See if there is any offensive way in me,
  and lead me in the way everlasting.

PSALM 139:1–2, 5–6, 14, 17, 23–24 (NIV 1984)

SEARCH ME, O GOD

1

Search me, O God, and know my heart.
PSALM 139:23 (NIV 1984)

"I hate restrictions, Lord. Clocks, calendars, commitments. Laws, diets, budgets. They are such a nuisance. So I squirm and wiggle to get free of them, but I only end up feeling even more restricted. I resist the very things you ordained to hold me together, and then I wonder why I feel as if I am coming apart. No wonder I feel anxious. Instead of stubbornly resolving to overcome my sin on my own, may I have the courage to ask you to 'Search me, O God.' Please show me the truth—that I am trying to hide behind anger and self-indulgence. Instead of wearily giving in to sin, may I take an honest look at what is making me most tired, for surely that is where I am putting up the biggest fight. May I not settle for the illusion of freedom I feel when I follow my instincts and emotions. I want the freedom that comes only when I let truth—your truth—be my best friend. For I know that only when I am honest about myself can I worship you in truth and gladness. Thank you that I need not fear being known—because I know that I am loved."

¹LORD, our Lord,
    how majestic is your name in all the earth!
You have set your glory
    in the heavens.
²Through the praise of children and infants
    you have established a stronghold against your
            enemies,
    to silence the foe and the avenger.
³When I consider your heavens,
    the work of your fingers,
the moon and the stars,
    which you have set in place,
⁴what is mankind that you are mindful of them,
    human beings that you care for them?
⁵You have made them a little lower than the angels
    and crowned them with glory and honor.
⁶You made them rulers over the works of your hands;
    you put everything under their feet:
⁷all flocks and herds,
    and the animals of the wild,
⁸the birds in the sky,
    and the fish in the sea,
    all that swim the paths of the seas.
⁹LORD, our Lord,
    how majestic is your name in all the earth!

PSALM 8

THE MAJESTY
OF YOUR NAME

2

*LORD, our Lord, how majestic
is your name in all the earth!*
PSALM 8:9

"The crown of glory and honor that you have placed upon our heads, Lord, often feels much too big. Like children playing dress-up we try to keep it on straight, but it keeps falling over our eyes. In our attempts to keep it in place, we realize one important thing: the One who put it there is the only One who can keep it there. And like a gentle father, you, the God of the universe, keep pushing it back in place so we can exercise our God-given authority over creation. The wonder of your plan calls me to silence. The majesty of your name calls me to kneel. And your awesome glory—the matchless glory of God—calls me to joyful worship."

¹Why, LORD, do you stand far off?
  Why do you hide yourself in times of trouble?
²In his arrogance the wicked man hunts down the weak,
  who are caught in the schemes he devises.
³He boasts about the cravings of his heart;
  he blesses the greedy and reviles the LORD.

⁶He says to himself, "Nothing will ever shake me."
  He swears, "No one will ever do me harm."

¹⁰His victims are crushed, they collapse;
  they fall under his strength.
¹¹He says to himself, "God will never notice;
  he covers his face and never sees."

¹⁴But you, God, see the trouble of the afflicted;
  you consider their grief and take it in hand.
The victims commit themselves to you;
  you are the helper of the fatherless.

¹⁶The LORD is King for ever and ever;
  the nations will perish from his land.
¹⁷You, LORD, hear the desire of the afflicted;
  you encourage them, and you listen to their cry.

PSALM 10:1–3, 6, 10–11, 14, 16–17

Rise Up and Sing

3

The LORD is King for ever and ever.
PSALM 10:16

"Heavenly Father, I think I am suffering from role reversal. Even though I call you 'Father,' I treat you like a child. I scold you if you don't respond immediately when I call. I punish you for creating situations that make it difficult for me to accomplish my plans. But then I recall your servant Job. His suffering was so severe that he cursed the day of his birth and asked you to remove it from the calendar.* He thought the world would be better if all memory of his life were erased. But you did the opposite of what he asked. Instead of removing all memory of him, you made sure he would be remembered forever. If Job had gotten what he asked for, we wouldn't have what we need—a story about suffering that helps us see our lives as part of something bigger than our situation. May we live each day in awe of what you are doing, not in anger over what you have not yet done. May we rise up today and sing of our great and glorious King!"

---

*See Job 3:1–11

¹Keep me safe, my God,
   for in you I take refuge.
²I say to the LORD, "You are my Lord;
   apart from you I have no good thing."

⁵LORD, you alone are my portion and my cup;
   you make my lot secure.
⁶The boundary lines have fallen for me in pleasant
      places;
   surely I have a delightful inheritance.
⁷I will praise the LORD, who counsels me;
   even at night my heart instructs me.
⁸I keep my eyes always on the LORD.
   With him at my right hand, I will not be shaken.
⁹Therefore my heart is glad and my tongue rejoices;
   my body also will rest secure,
¹⁰because you will not abandon me to the realm of the
      dead,
   nor will you let your faithful one see decay.
¹¹You make known to me the path of life;
   you will fill me with joy in your presence,
   with eternal pleasures at your right hand.

PSALM 16:1–2, 5–11

¹⁵As for me, I will be vindicated and will see your face;
   when I awake, I will be satisfied with seeing your
      likeness.

PSALM 17:15

WONDERFUL NEWS

I keep my eyes always on the LORD.
With him at my right hand, I will not be shaken.
Therefore my heart is glad and my tongue rejoices;
my body also will rest secure.
PSALM 16:8–9

"When I awake to the morning news instead of your Holy Word, Lord, why am I surprised that I don't see you? When I spend so much time focused on the evil in this world, is it any wonder that I see so little of your goodness? This morning I want to set aside my idea of a perfect situation so I can see your perfect face. I want to turn my back on sin and turn my heart toward you. For me, this act of repentance is only one small step—like a simple pivot from east to west—but you offer to take that small move and turn it into a giant step by taking my sin as far from me as the east is from the west.* This is indeed wonderful news, Lord! And it clarifies my calling. I don't have to point out everything that's wrong; I just have to turn away from it and point toward what is good with words of truth and deeds of love."

---

*See Psalm 103:12

[1] Vindicate me, my God,
  and plead my cause
  against an unfaithful nation.
Rescue me from those who are
  deceitful and wicked.
[2] You are God my stronghold.
  Why have you rejected me?
Why must I go about mourning,
  oppressed by the enemy?
[3] Send me your light and your faithful care;
  let them lead me;
let them bring me to your holy mountain,
  to the place where you dwell.
[4] Then I will go to the altar of God,
  to God, my joy and my delight.
I will praise you with the lyre,
  O God, my God.

PSALM 43:1–4

YOUR CLEAR LIGHT OF TRUTH

5

Send out your light and your truth!
PSALM 43:3 (TLB)

"During those times when I want to celebrate your nearness, Lord, why do you sometimes seem so distant? When I try so hard to create happiness, why do I lose so much joy? In this world in which you are the light, why is there so much darkness? And when I want so much to experience your goodness, why does evil show up at my doorstep? May I learn anew that I cannot work my way into your presence. Remind me that I cannot buy my way into your favor. Help me understand that I cannot reach you by taking shortcuts through darkness. And teach me again that I cannot build walls high enough to protect myself from evil. I want to follow your clear light of truth, reach your holy mountain, and praise you for being King of kings and Lord of lords."

¹Hear this, all you peoples;
   listen, all who live in this world,
²both low and high,
   rich and poor alike:
³My mouth will speak words of wisdom;
   the meditation of my heart will give you
      understanding.
⁴I will turn my ear to a proverb;
   with the harp I will expound my riddle:
⁵Why should I fear when evil days come,
   when wicked deceivers surround me—
⁶those who trust in their wealth
   and boast of their great riches?
⁷No man can redeem the life of another
   or give to God a ransom for them—
⁸the ransom for a life is costly,
   no payment is ever enough.

¹⁵But God will redeem me from the realm of the dead;
   he will surely take me to himself.

PSALM 49:1–8, 15

I Have Everything I Need

6

Why should I fear when evil days come,
when wicked deceivers surround me—
those who trust in their wealth
and boast of their great riches?
PSALM 49:5–6

"Forgive me, Lord, for thinking that to do your will I need anything more than what you have given: my own hands to extend the love and kindness you want to give, my own feet to take me where you want to go, and my own story of redemption to explain your will for the world. Forgive me for waiting for better circumstances, more talent, more time, or a bigger budget. Forgive me for trying to manipulate circumstances to accomplish my will rather than yours. I am grateful that you are redeeming me from the foolish ways of the world, and I want my life to be evidence of your transforming power. May I live every day in the awareness that I have everything I need to accomplish whatever you want me to do. Lord, help me take advantage of every situation I'm in to lift up the name of Jesus."

¹Why do you boast of evil, you mighty hero? . . .
²You who practice deceit,
   your tongue plots destruction;
   it is like a sharpened razor.
³You love evil rather than good,
   falsehood rather than speaking the truth.

⁵Surely God will bring you down to everlasting ruin:
   He will snatch you up and pluck you from your tent;
   he will uproot you from the land of the living.
⁶The righteous will see and fear;
   they will laugh at you, saying,
⁷"Here now is the man
   who did not make God his stronghold
but trusted in his great wealth
   and grew strong by destroying others!"
⁸But I am like an olive tree
   flourishing in the house of God;
I trust in God's unfailing love
   for ever and ever.
⁹For what you have done I will always praise you
   in the presence of your faithful people.
And I will hope in your name,
   for your name is good.

PSALM 52

FORGIVE ME, LORD

7

I am like an olive tree flourishing
in the house of God;
I trust in God's unfailing love
for ever and ever.
PSALM 52:8

"Father, forgive me for thinking of life as a commodity I can give or take in trade for something I'd rather have. Forgive me for refusing to learn the lesson of dependence that you teach through children. Forgive me for shutting my mind to truth and closing my heart to love. Forgive me for thinking that I can get rid of guilt by destroying something good. Forgive me for believing liars who practice deceit and plot the destruction of the innocent and helpless. Forgive me for choosing to destroy with words or deeds the good you have chosen to create. Forgive me for stifling voices of praise. Thank you for breath. May I use it only to praise you. Thank you for life. May I use it only to exalt you."

^{10}Create in me a pure heart, O God,
   and renew a steadfast spirit within me.
^{11}Do not cast me from your presence
   or take your Holy Spirit from me.
^{12}Restore to me the joy of your salvation
   and grant me a willing spirit, to sustain me.

^{15}Open my lips, Lord,
   and my mouth will declare your praise.
^{16}You do not delight in sacrifice, or I would bring it;
   you do not take pleasure in burnt offerings.
^{17}My sacrifice, O God, is a broken spirit;
   a broken and contrite heart
   you, God, will not despise.

PSALM 51:10–12, 15–17

SOUL MATES: FORGIVENESS AND CONFESSION

8

A broken and contrite heart you, God,
will not despise.
PSALM 51:17

"By being involved in churches for many years I've learned how to make myself acceptable to other believers: just do what's expected. But I know that doesn't make me acceptable to you, Lord. I've been slow to learn that you are more interested in the 'why' of my behavior than the 'what.' And I've hesitated to realize that my service for you is meaningless if my motive is to get people to think well of me rather than you. But little by little I am learning that spiritual health comes not from making myself stronger but from acknowledging my weakness. And I'm discovering that happiness comes not in looking for ways to perfect my image but in finding ways to reflect yours. I am learning that forgiveness and confession are soul mates and that I can't enjoy the freedom found in the company of forgiveness without entertaining that annoying companion called 'confession.' Open my eyes, Lord, so I can see that the only way to find you is to stay on the road called holiness with companions named Confession and Forgiveness."

⁵Be exalted, O God, above the heavens;
  let your glory be over all the earth.
⁶They spread a net for my feet—
  I was bowed down in distress.
They dug a pit in my path—
  but they have fallen into it themselves.
⁷My heart, O God, is steadfast,
  my heart is steadfast;
  I will sing and make music.
⁸Awake, my soul!
  Awake, harp and lyre!
  I will awaken the dawn.
⁹I will praise you, Lord, among the nations;
  I will sing of you among the peoples.
¹⁰For great is your love, reaching to the heavens;
  your faithfulness reaches to the skies.
¹¹Be exalted, O God, above the heavens;
  let your glory be over all the earth.

PSALM 57:5–11

AWAKEN MY SOUL, O LORD

9

Awake, my soul! . . . I will praise you,
Lord, among the nations.
PSALM 57:8–9

"Awaken my soul, Lord, with the glory of your presence. Awaken my heart to the music of praise. May I cast off my cozy blankets and crawl out of my comfortable bed before the alarm clock of crisis sounds. Clothe me with power from on high so I will be ready to take up the cause of eternity—not be taken in by the pull of earthly pleasures. I am so much like the Israelites of old, who so joyously celebrated your victories on their behalf but who so reluctantly went to battle on behalf of anyone else. May I look to the heavens, Lord, as a reminder that your love surrounds the whole earth. May I see in the sky your faithfulness to everyone it covers. May the praise of your redeemed people everywhere blanket the earth with your glory. May our collective worship express our willingness to exalt your name in all the world."

^{1}Truly my soul finds rest in God;
   my salvation comes from him.
^{2}Truly he is my rock and my salvation;
   he is my fortress, I will never be shaken.
^{3}How long will you assault me?
   Would all of you throw me down—
   this leaning wall, this tottering fence?
^{4}Surely they intend to topple me
   from my lofty place;
   they take delight in lies.
With their mouths they bless,
   but in their hearts they curse.
^{5}Yes, my soul, find rest in God;
   my hope comes from him.
^{6}Truly he is my rock and my salvation;
   he is my fortress, I will not be shaken.
^{7}My salvation and my honor depend on God;
   he is my mighty rock, my refuge.
^{8}Trust in him at all times, you people;
   pour out your hearts to him,
   for God is our refuge.

PSALM 62:1–8

HERE TO WORSHIP

10

Yes, my soul, find rest in God;
my hope comes from him.
Truly he is my rock and my salvation;
he is my fortress, I will not be shaken.
PSALM 62:5–6

"I go to church to worship you, Lord, but I'm not very good at it. The reason is not because our style of worship is too formal or informal; it's not because we have the wrong mix of hymns and praise songs; it's not because I can't hear the accompaniment or see the song leader. The reason I fail to worship is because I don't hear and see you! I don't hear you because I don't take time to stop and listen, and I don't see you because my heart is impure. I spend too much energy trying to get everything around me changed to reflect my idea of perfection and not enough time resting in your ability to make all things perfect. Instead of trying to accomplish in others what only you can do, may I cooperate with you in what you are doing in me. Then I will be able to see you in all your glory and sing of your wonderful love."

⁴Blessed are those you choose
    and bring near to live in your courts!
We are filled with the good things of your house,
    of your holy temple.
⁵You answer us with awesome and righteous deeds,
    God our Savior,
the hope of all the ends of the earth
    and of the farthest seas,
⁶who formed the mountains by your power,
    having armed yourself with strength,
⁷who stilled the roaring of the seas,
    the roaring of their waves,
    and the turmoil of the nations.
⁸The whole earth is filled with awe at your wonders;
    where morning dawns, where evening fades,
    you call forth songs of joy.

PSALM 65:4–8

My Frantic Pursuit

11

The whole earth is filled with awe
at your wonders; where morning dawns,
where evening fades, you call forth songs of joy.
PSALM 65:8

"Thank you, Lord, that all of your gifts are good. Thank you that you know what I need even when I don't know myself. Forgive me for rejecting what you say is good in my frantic pursuit of something I think is better. I know how it feels when someone I care about doesn't appreciate the gifts I give, and I wonder if that's how you feel when I refuse your gift of rest. The fact that I consider rest a burden rather than a blessing tells me how much different my thoughts are from yours. You say that my willingness to rest from work will be a sign to others that you are with me,* but I live as if have to prove your presence by the work I do. Help me to see that my dependence on work is an attempt to prove my own importance, not yours. With my lips I call you 'king of creation,' but I behave as if the creating I do in my work is more important than the re-creating you do in me through rest. May I stop trying to prove myself to others through work and begin letting you prove yourself to me through rest. Then I will know that you are indeed my health and salvation. Then I will be able to join all creation in glad adoration."

---

*See Matthew 11:28–30

¹In you, Lord, I have taken refuge;
   let me never be put to shame.
²In your righteousness, rescue me and deliver me;
   turn your ear to me and save me.
³Be my rock of refuge,
   to which I can always go;
give the command to save me,
   for you are my rock and my fortress.
⁴Deliver me, my God, from the hand of the wicked,
   from the grasp of those who are evil and cruel.
⁵For you have been my hope, Sovereign Lord,
   my confidence since my youth.
⁶From birth I have relied on you;
   you brought me forth from my mother's womb.
   I will ever praise you.
⁷I have become a sign to many;
   you are my strong refuge.
⁸My mouth is filled with your praise,
   declaring your splendor all day long.

PSALM 71:1–8

A Refuge from Trouble

12

Be my rock of refuge, to which I can always go;
give the command to save me,
for you are my rock and my fortress.
PSALM 71:3

"Thank you, Father, for being our refuge from trouble. Thank you for being our deliverer when we follow the light of your truth and take up residence on the rock of your love. May we build our homes on the sure foundation of loving trust and honesty so we will not be put to shame. Please give our children a reason to rejoice by making their homes a safe and loving place where they see a true picture of who you are and how much you love them. May our church be a safe refuge for those who are helpless and a shining light for those who feel hopelessly lost. May we be fully persuaded that the power of your love is able to repair any relationship and that every good gift is within your ability to give. May we lift your name on high as we declare your splendor all day long."

[1-5]No doubt about it! God is good—
  good to good people, good to the
      good-hearted.
But I nearly missed it,
  missed seeing his goodness.
I was looking the other way,
  looking up to the people
At the top,
  envying the wicked who have it made . . .

[11-20] . . . The wicked get by with everything;
  they have it made, piling up riches.
I've been stupid to play by the rules;
  what has it gotten me?
A long run of bad luck, that's what—
  a slap in the face every time I walk out the door.
If I'd have given in and talked like this,
  I would have betrayed your dear children.
Still, when I tried to figure it out,
  all I got was a splitting headache . . .
Until I entered the sanctuary of God.
  Then I saw the whole picture.

[24-28]You wisely and tenderly lead me,
  and then you bless me.
You're all I want in heaven!
  You're all I want on earth! . . .
Look! Those who left you are falling apart!
  Deserters, they'll never be heard from again.
But I'm in the very presence of GOD—
  oh, how refreshing it is!

PSALM 73:1–5, 11–20, 24–28 (MSG)

SANCTUARY

13

I'm in the very presence of God—
oh, how refreshing it is!
PSALM 73:27 (MSG)

"Thank you, Father, that you have provided a place where I can bring all my doubts and fears, all my anger and confusion—right here to your sanctuary.* Forgive me for thinking of the local church as the place where I must prove that I am strong rather than admit that I am weak. Forgive me for using my church as a place to give pat answers rather than to acknowledge difficult questions. Forgive me for using it as a place to prove my own worth rather than as a place to see you demonstrate yours. Forgive me for thinking of it as a place where everyone is perfect rather than as a place where imperfect people meet to celebrate your generous mercy and perfect love. Thank you for this place where I can be a child again. Make me trusting and eager to learn, not stubborn and convinced that I already know it all. Make me childlike in my faith as I praise you for being the strongest Dad of all."

---

*See Psalm 73:17

¹I will sing of the LORD's great love forever;
    with my mouth I will make your faithfulness known
    through all generations.
²I will declare that your love stands firm forever,
    that you have established your faithfulness in heaven
        itself.

⁵The heavens praise your wonders, LORD,
    your faithfulness too, in the assembly of the holy
        ones.
⁶For who in the skies above can compare with the
        LORD?
    Who is like the LORD among the heavenly beings?
⁷In the council of the holy ones God is greatly feared;
    he is more awesome than all who surround him.
⁸Who is like you, LORD God Almighty?
    You, LORD, are mighty, and your faithfulness
        surrounds you.

¹⁴Righteousness and justice are the foundation of your
        throne;
    love and faithfulness go before you.
¹⁵Blessed are those who have learned to acclaim you,
    who walk in the light of your presence, LORD.
¹⁶They rejoice in your name all day long;
    they celebrate your righteousness.

PSALM 89:1–2, 5–8, 14–16

THE MUSIC OF MY LIFE

I will sing of the LORD's great love forever;
with my mouth I will make your
faithfulness known through all generations.
PSALM 89:1

"Sometimes I forget, Lord, that my life is a song and that you are the composer. Sometimes I forget that I am your instrument and that you are the musician. How foolish of me to think I can make music apart from you. How arrogant to think I know the right notes to play or the right time to play them. May I be faithful in submitting myself to your direction so no one will doubt that the music of my life comes from above, not from within. May the song of my life be the melody of your love. May I continually lift my voice to proclaim your faithfulness, to exalt your holy name, and to rejoice in your coming kingdom."

⁵The heavens praise your wonders, LORD,
  your faithfulness too, in the assembly of the holy
      ones.
⁶For who in the skies above can compare with the
  LORD?
  Who is like the LORD among the heavenly beings?

¹¹The heavens are yours, and yours also the earth;
  you founded the world and all that is in it.
¹²You created the north and the south;
  Tabor and Hermon sing for joy at your name.

¹⁴Righteousness and justice are the foundation of your
      throne;
  love and faithfulness go before you.
¹⁵Blessed are those who have learned to acclaim you,
  who walk in the light of your presence, LORD.

¹⁷For you are their glory and strength,
  and by your favor you exalt our horn.
¹⁸Indeed, our shield belongs to the LORD,
  our king to the Holy One of Israel.

PSALM 89:5–6, 11–12, 14–15, 17–18

Exalt Jesus's Name

15

The heavens praise your wonders, LORD,
your faithfulness too.
PSALM 89:5

"Thank you, heavenly Father, that you chose to ride a plodding donkey rather than a speeding steed.* Thank you that even a simple gift becomes great when it is given in your name. Thank you that even the nameless are remembered when they glorify your name. Too often, though, I am like those who welcomed you with shouts of praise when they thought you were going to save them from the tyranny of Rome but soon were cursing you because you upset their religious leaders rather than their political oppressors.** Like them, I too would rather be ruled by one who imposes laws than by One who exposes sin. Change my thinking, Lord. May I stop trying to suppress my sin with human effort and accept with childlike faith the divine effort of your Son, who chose not to suppress sin but to conquer it. He did so not by raising himself to be our king but by lowering himself to be our sacrifice. No wonder His name is exalted. No wonder He deserves all praise!"

*See Matthew 21:5–7
**See Matthew 21:9 and Matthew 27:19–22

¹Come, let us sing for joy to the LORD;
   let us shout aloud to the Rock of our salvation.
²Let us come before him with thanksgiving
   and extol him with music and song.
³For the LORD is the great God,
   the great King above all gods.
⁴In his hand are the depths of the earth,
   and the mountain peaks belong to him.
⁵The sea is his, for he made it,
   and his hands formed the dry land.
⁶Come, let us bow down in worship,
   let us kneel before the LORD our Maker;
⁷for he is our God
   and we are the people of his pasture,
   the flock under his care.

PSALM 95:1–7

TIME TO REFOCUS

16

Come, let us bow down in worship,
let us kneel before the LORD our Maker.
PSALM 95:6

"Day after day, Lord, I see the tragic results of anger, jealousy, and hatred, yet still I allow seeds of these thoughts and attitudes to remain in my heart and mind. Day after day I hear the gods of power, prestige, wealth, and self-righteousness calling me to bow down to them, and sometimes I do. Day after day I make decisions as to whether I will further my own agenda or yours, whether I will exalt my name or yours, whether I will help the enemy in his rampage of hatred and darkness or build your kingdom of love and light. Thank you, Lord, for time to refocus, to take my eyes off the evils of this world and Satan's strategy of destruction, and to be reminded of the goodness of your kingdom and your strategy of redemption. Thank you for the assurance that I am in your care—and so is the entire world! Thank you for the privilege of coming into your presence and singing your praise."

¹Sing to the LORD a new song,
    for he has done marvelous things;
his right hand and his holy arm
    have worked salvation for him.

⁴Shout for joy to the LORD, all the earth,
    burst into jubilant song with music;
⁵make music to the LORD with the harp,
    with the harp and the sound of singing,
⁶with trumpets and the blast of the ram's horn—
    shout for joy before the LORD, the King.
⁷Let the sea resound, and everything in it,
    the world, and all who live in it.
⁸Let the rivers clap their hands,
    let the mountains sing together for joy.

PSALM 98:1, 4–8

SACRIFICE OF CONFESSION 17

Let the rivers clap their hands,
let the mountains sing together for joy.
PSALM 98:8

"I know this may sound childish, Lord, but those rivers of yours that clap and the mountains that sing have all the fun. If all I had to do was tell about your greatness, I'd be happy too. I love confessing who you are; it's confessing who I am that ruins my day. I enjoy singing about wanting to know you and be like you, but 'living it' wears me down. I continually resist doing what will make me more like you, and I refuse to admit when that happens. Confession is scary! Once I start, I will lose control over where I go. Week after week I happily bring into our house of worship my sacrifice of praise for what you have done. So now I humbly bring my sacrifice of confession for the wrong I have done. I do it with fear and trembling, Lord, but also with confidence that it will bring joy to your heart, peace to my church family, and love to the world. The sacrifice of confession is certainly something worth shouting about!"

¹Praise the LORD, my soul;
   all my inmost being, praise his holy name.
²Praise the LORD, my soul,
   and forget not all his benefits—
³who forgives all your sins
   and heals all your diseases,
⁴who redeems your life from the pit
   and crowns you with love and compassion,
⁵who satisfies your desires with good things
   so that your youth is renewed like the eagle's.

⁸The LORD is compassionate and gracious,
   slow to anger, abounding in love.

¹¹For as high as the heavens are above the earth,
   so great is his love for those who fear him;

¹⁹The LORD has established his throne in heaven,
   and his kingdom rules over all.

²²Praise the LORD, all his works
   everywhere in his dominion.
Praise the LORD, my soul.

PSALM 103:1–5, 8, 11, 19, 22

SAFE WITH YOU

Praise the LORD, my soul;
all my inmost being, praise his holy name.
Praise the LORD, my soul,
and forget not all his benefits.
PSALM 103:1–2

"Sometimes life hurts so much, Lord, that I try to relieve my emotional pain by doing something to make someone else feel bad. Sometimes it's so much trouble to think about what I should do that I just go ahead and do what is the least amount of trouble. And sometimes it's too much work to do the right thing, so I just make myself feel good about doing the wrong thing. We all have our coping mechanisms, O Father. We all have our safe places and our danger zones. Some of us feel safer in the mental realm, some in the world of emotions, and some in the 'just get it done' mode. But none of those places is safe if you are excluded. We are made in your image, Lord. We are meant to be thinkers, feelers, and doers; yet so often we get ourselves in trouble by letting these areas get out of balance. May we not trust good feelings that are based on lies. May we not wield truth without feeling love. May we not undertake grandiose plans without knowing and understanding and loving the architect of the universe. Almighty King, Incarnate Word, Holy Comforter, I know that my ways, my thoughts, and my desires are all safe with you, so I praise you in this moment with all my mind and soul and strength."

[1] My heart, O God, is steadfast;
   I will sing and make music with all my soul.
[2] Awake, harp and lyre!
   I will awaken the dawn.
[3] I will praise you, LORD, among the nations;
   I will sing of you among the peoples.
[4] For great is your love, higher than the heavens;
   your faithfulness reaches to the skies.
[5] Be exalted, O God, above the heavens;
   let your glory be over all the earth.

PSALM 108:1–5

More about You, Lord

19

Be exalted, O God, above the heavens;
let your glory be over all the earth.
PSALM 108:5

"I know, Lord, that more important than the words we sing at church is the life we lead during the week. More important than the emotion I feel while worshiping in song with my brothers and sisters in Christ is the motive that drives me after I leave the building. The music I make with the air I breathe is only a symbol of the music made with my soul. Thank you, Father, for the miracle of music, which takes something as simple as air and, through obedience to the laws of nature, transforms it into melodies and harmonies that lift up my spirit. How great you are for creating something so complex and yet making it so simple for us to enjoy. Thank you, Father, for the miracle of your love, which takes something as simple as my everyday experiences and, through obedience to your Word, transforms them into a life of praise that exalts your name above the heavens and spreads your glory over all the earth."

¹I will exalt you, my God the King;
  I will praise your name for ever and ever.
²Every day I will praise you
  and extol your name for ever and ever.
³Great is the LORD and most worthy of praise;
  his greatness no one can fathom.
⁴One generation commends your works to another;
  they tell of your mighty acts.

⁷They celebrate your abundant goodness
  and joyfully sing of your righteousness.
⁸The LORD is gracious and compassionate,
  slow to anger and rich in love.
⁹The LORD is good to all;
  he has compassion on all he has made.
¹⁰All your works praise you, LORD;
  your faithful people extol you.
¹¹They tell of the glory of your kingdom
  and speak of your might,
¹²so that all people may know of your mighty acts
  and the glorious splendor of your kingdom.

PSALM 145:1–4, 7–12

A CELEBRATION
OF YOUR PROVISION

The LORD is good to all;
he has compassion on all he has made.
PSALM 145:9

"How quickly I forget the goodness of your creation when a few days of rain spoil my vacation. How quickly I question your love when you refuse to use your power to make people please me. How easily I forget that others have needs when I don't yet have everything I want. Forgive me, Lord, for my self-centeredness. Open my eyes to the wonders surrounding me. May I enjoy your blessings without cursing others through thoughtless spending, meaningless accumulation, and selfish consumption. May I find joy and meaning in giving to others from the abundance you have given to me. May every meal I eat be a celebration of your provision, may every delightful sensation I feel be a reminder of your delight in my pleasure, and may every sound I make be a song of praise for your greatness."

¹Give thanks to the LORD, for he is good;
   his love endures forever.

⁶The LORD is with me; I will not be afraid.
   What can mere mortals do to me?

⁸It is better to take refuge in the LORD
   than to trust in humans.

¹⁴The LORD is my strength and my defense;
   he has become my salvation.
¹⁵Shouts of joy and victory
   resound in the tents of the righteous:

²⁵LORD, save us!
   LORD, grant us success!
²⁶Blessed is he who comes in the name of the LORD.
   From the house of the LORD we bless you.

PSALM 118:1, 6, 8, 14–15, 25–26

YOUR GOODNESS, LORD, NOT MINE

21

Give thanks to the LORD, for he is good;
his love endures forever.
PSALM 118:1

"I know, Lord, that Satan would have me believe that being silent is the same as being strong and that having no conflict is the same as living in peace. But I know that neither is necessarily true. While giving the illusion of being good and right, those situations can be deceptively wrong. Failing to speak words that need to be heard can be just as destructive as speaking the wrong words, and avoiding conflict can be just as damaging as causing it. I know, Lord, that true success is not getting more people to conform to my will, it's inspiring people to be transformed by yours. And I know that true victory is letting you overcome my sin—not using other people to help me disguise it. I want to depend on your strength, Father, not my schemes. I want to display your goodness, Lord, not prove my own. And I want your love to be my fortress, O God, not my accomplishments."

¹Out of the depths I cry to you, LORD;
  ²Lord, hear my voice.
Let your ears be attentive
  to my cry for mercy.
³If you, LORD, kept a record of sins,
  Lord, who could stand?
⁴But with you there is forgiveness,
  so that we can, with reverence, serve you.
⁵I wait for the LORD, my whole being waits,
  and in his word I put my hope.
⁶I wait for the Lord
  more than watchmen wait for the morning,
  more than watchmen wait for the morning.
⁷Israel, put your hope in the LORD,
  for with the LORD is unfailing love
  and with him is full redemption.
⁸He himself will redeem Israel
  from all their sins.

PSALM 130

Reign in My Life

22

If you, LORD, kept a record of sins, Lord,
who could stand? But with you there is forgiveness,
so that we can, with reverence, serve you.
PSALM 130:3–4

"The clutter in my house proves that I have trouble letting go of things, Lord, and I know that is not good. But what about all the good things you have put into my life? Is it wrong for me to want to hold onto them? Perhaps in trying to make you seem more real, I've allowed your gifts to become more important to me than you are. Maybe what I do for you has become more important to me than what you want to do for me. I want to feel your presence, Lord, but maybe I've been trying too hard to create it with the work I do. I want to experience your love, but maybe I've been trying too hard to earn it from others. I'm sorry, but I'm also sad. I believe that you reign in heaven, but I long for the day when you also will reign in my life and on all the earth."

¹I cry aloud to the LORD;
   I lift up my voice to the LORD for mercy.
²I pour out before him my complaint;
   before him I tell my trouble.
³When my spirit grows faint within me,
   it is you who watch over my way.
In the path where I walk
   people have hidden a snare for me.
⁴Look and see, there is no one at my right hand;
   no one is concerned for me.
I have no refuge;
   no one cares for my life.
⁵I cry to you, LORD;
   I say, "You are my refuge,
   my portion in the land of the living."
⁶Listen to my cry,
   for I am in desperate need;
rescue me from those who pursue me,
   for they are too strong for me.
⁷Set me free from my prison,
   that I may praise your name.
Then the righteous will gather about me
   because of your goodness to me.

PSALM 142

LEAVING MESSAGES

Listen to my cry,
for I am in desperate need.
PSALM 142:6

"When I leave messages for others, Lord, I expect to receive an answer. When I don't, I assume the worst—that I've done something bad, that someone is mad at me, or that I am no longer loved. But usually I am wrong, and most of the time the reason doesn't even involve me at all. I know, Lord, that I am like this with you too. When I don't get an immediate answer from you, I assume that you're giving me the silent treatment to punish me for something I've done wrong. But you do not get angry when I cry for help nor do you punish me for my lack of faith. You are quiet—not to punish me but to get my attention. And the reason I often don't hear you is that I'm too busy filling the air with nervous conversation. Thank you, Father, for listening to me. Forgive me for not listening to you. Thank you for being patient with me. Forgive me for being impatient with you. Thank you for never misjudging my motives. Forgive me for misjudging yours. Help me to remember that faith is what I receive as a result of being obedient—not something you give to make obedience easy. May I not expect you to rescue me so I can gloat over my enemies but so my enemies might become your friends. Thank you that my many fears can never diminish your love and that my many tears cannot extinguish gladness when I place my hope in you."

[1] Rescue me, LORD, from evildoers;
    protect me from the violent,
[2] who devise evil plans in their hearts
    and stir up war every day.
[3] They make their tongues as sharp as a serpent's;
    the poison of vipers is on their lips.
[4] Keep me safe, LORD, from the hands of the wicked;
    protect me from the violent,
    who devise ways to trip my feet.
[5] The arrogant have hidden a snare for me;
    they have spread out the cords of their net
    and have set traps for me along my path.
[6] I say to the LORD, "You are my God."
    Hear, LORD, my cry for mercy.
[7] Sovereign LORD, my strong deliverer,
    you shield my head in the day of battle.

[13] Surely the righteous will praise your name,
    and the upright will live in your presence.

PSALM 140:1–7, 13

Victory over Sin

24

Rescue me, LORD, from evildoers;
protect me from the violent,
who devise evil plans in their hearts
and stir up war every day.
PSALM 140:1

"Father, I suppose I could consider gravity a problem—it keeps me from doing something I want to do. I suppose I could consider a mountain a nuisance—it keeps me from getting where I want to go. I suppose I could call a river stubborn because it flows only in one direction. But if I were to make all of those accusations, I would only be admitting my own foolishness. Yet that is what I do when I resist the way things are simply because they're not the way I want them to be. I want to finish the journey we've started, Lord, but I know by how weary I get that I'm carrying more stuff than I need. All of it seems important for survival, so I'm a little concerned about walking away from it. I've got all these words I can use to stop those who disagree with me. I've got my temper when my words are ignored. I've got sarcasm and ridicule when intimidation fails. So maybe the reason I have no victory over my enemies is because so much of the enemy is still in me. Lord, help me to remember that the most important victory is not over other people but over my own sin, and never let me forget that the victory over sin comes only through the mercy of your Son."

[1]Praise the LORD.
How good it is to sing praises to our God,
how pleasant and fitting to praise him!

[4]He determines the number of the stars
and calls them each by name.
[5]Great is our Lord and mighty in power;
his understanding has no limit.

[11]The LORD delights in those who fear him,
who put their hope in his unfailing love.

PSALM 147:1, 4–5, 11

MY LIFE; GOD'S PLANS

25

The LORD delights in those who fear him,
who put their hope in his unfailing love.
PSALM 147:11

"Thank you, dear Father, for filling the heavens with proof of your mighty power, for if all I had was my own strength I would live in constant fear. Thank you for placing so many indescribably beautiful things at my fingertips as evidence of your unlimited understanding. If all I had was my own knowledge, I would live in constant confusion. And thank you for putting your pledge of love into writing. If all I had was my own experience, I would get seasick riding the waves of faith and doubt. Forgive me for listening to messages that say my value is measured by how much I do for you, for you say that my value is based on what you do for me. When I feel as if I am failing because I cannot accomplish everything in my daily planner, remind me that the only important thing is that you are accomplishing your plan in my life. I know, Lord, that each small step of obedience leads me further into the greatness of your kingdom. And I know that there is nothing greater than living in the shelter of your unfailing love."

¹Blessed is the one
     who does not walk in step with the wicked
or stand in the way that sinners take
     or sit in the company of mockers,
²but whose delight is in the law of the LORD,
     and who meditates on his law day and night.

PSALM 1:1–2

I Abandon My Life

Blessed is the one . . . whose delight is in the law of the LORD.
PSALM 1:1–2

"I pray for your kingdom to come, Lord, but often I refuse to let it into my own heart. I pray for your will to be done, but often I refuse to do it. I say I want peace in the world, but I am often the cause of conflict here at home among my family, friends, and fellow believers. I say that I agree with you, but I sometimes use more energy trying to convince you to do my will than I do trying to carry out yours. Forgive me for trying to remake the world into my idea of perfection rather than working with you to restore it to your original design. May my praise today become my pledge that I have abandoned my life to your holy calling."

¹Lord, who may dwell in your sacred tent?
    Who may live on your holy mountain?
²The one whose walk is blameless,
    who does what is righteous,
    who speaks the truth from their heart;
³whose tongue utters no slander,
    who does no wrong to a neighbor,
    and casts no slur on others;
⁴who despises a vile person
    but honors those who fear the Lord;
who keeps an oath even when it hurts,
    and does not change their mind;
⁵who lends money to the poor without interest;
    who does not accept a bribe against the innocent.
Whoever does these things
    will never be shaken.

PSALM 15

THE KINGDOM I LONG FOR! 27

LORD, who may dwell in your sacred tent?
Who may live on your holy mountain?
The one whose walk is blameless,
who does what is righteous,
who speaks the truth from their heart."
PSALM 15:1–2

"O, Lord, if my walk has to be blameless, I am in big trouble, for I sometimes twist truth to favor my circumstances. I often imply bad things about people to make myself seem innocent. And I've been known to rationalize my way out of commitments whenever they become difficult. But I know, Lord, that your way is better. So today I turn my heart toward you and pray that my behavior will follow. I long to be free from the manmade laws that can be manipulated to favor the guilty, so I abandon myself to your laws, which are impartial and unchanging. I am tired of trying to justify myself by condemning others, so today I will look into your Word to see the truth about my own sin, not anyone else's. And I long to be done with the ways of mortals, which rely on foolish arguments, childish name-calling, and spiritual shoving in an effort to earn a position closer to you. I submit myself to your way alone, which rests completely on love. This is the kingdom I long for. This is the kingdom you are preparing me for. This is the kingdom I praise you for."

¹I love you, LORD, my strength.
²The LORD is my rock, my fortress and my deliverer;
   my God is my rock, in whom I take refuge,
   my shield and the horn of my salvation,
   my stronghold.
³I called to the LORD, who is worthy of praise,
   and I have been saved from my enemies.

⁴⁶The LORD lives! Praise be to my Rock!
   Exalted be God my Savior!
⁴⁷He is the God who avenges me,
   who subdues nations under me,
      ⁴⁸who saves me from my enemies.
You exalted me above my foes;
   from a violent man you rescued me.
⁴⁹Therefore I will praise you, LORD, among the nations;
   I will sing the praises of your name.

PSALM 18:1–3, 46–49

Why Do I Settle?

The LORD is my rock,
my fortress and my deliverer;
my God is my rock,
in whom I take refuge,
my shield and the horn of my salvation,
my stronghold.
PSALM 18:2

"I ask you, God, for a slight attitude adjustment, but you want to change my mind. I ask you for better circumstances, O Sovereign One, but you want to make me a better person. I ask you, Lord, to remove me from the discomfort my sin has caused, but you want to remove my sin. I ask you, dear Father, to help me fit in with my friends, but you want me to stand out for your glory. Why do I settle for alteration when you offer transformation? Why do I settle for safety when you promise victory? Why do I settle for the world when I can have you, almighty God?"

²⁷ All the ends of the earth
    will remember and turn to the LORD,
and all the families of the nations
    will bow down before him,
²⁸ for dominion belongs to the LORD
    and he rules over the nations.

PSALM 22:27–28

Under God's Righteous Rule

*All the ends of the earth will
remember and turn to the LORD.*
PSALM 22:27

"Thank you, Father, for allowing us to participate in electing those who rule our nation, but thank you even more for electing us to one day rule in heaven. Every four years when we as Americans cast ballots for what some say is the most powerful position in the world, we know that true power comes not from being elected president of the United States but from being chosen as one of your children. Yes, it is important to have God-fearing rulers in our nation, but it is more important to have the love of God ruling in our hearts. We have heard candidates promise to fight for us, but to do so they will have to defeat some of us. What a wonderful difference in your kingdom, Lord, for you did all the losing so we could all be winners! What a marvelous privilege to be under your righteous rule! What an amazing promise to know that one day all your creatures will again recognize and submit to your authority! Alleluia!"

^{1}The earth is the LORD's, and everything in it,
   the world, and all who live in it;
^{2}for he founded it on the seas
   and established it on the waters.

^{7}Lift up your heads, you gates;
   be lifted up, you ancient doors,
   that the King of glory may come in.
^{8}Who is this King of glory?
   The LORD strong and mighty,
   the LORD mighty in battle.
^{9}Lift up your heads, you gates;
   lift them up, you ancient doors,
   that the King of glory may come in.
^{10}Who is he, this King of glory?
   The LORD Almighty—
   he is the King of glory.

PSALM 24:1–2, 7–10

CHANGE MY DESIRE

3O

Who is he, this King of glory?
The LORD Almighty—
he is the King of glory.
PSALM 24:10

"Lord Almighty, King of glory, I am ashamed to admit how often I call on your name to ask you to make life easier for me in the natural world rather than to make me stronger in the spiritual world. Keep me from thinking that your name, O God, is a magic word I can use to invoke divine power for my own comfort and convenience. Teach me instead that it is a holy word meant to unleash the power of truth and love against the forces of evil. How is it, Lord, that demons know your name is 'Holy One,' but I still call you health, wealth, and success? How is it that evil spirits obey you, but I still try to get you to obey me? Change my desire for earthly power and control into a longing for spiritual victory over selfishness and pride. I lift my face to you today so your glory may come into my life. May the glory of your presence be recognized in me just as it was in Jesus when He walked this earth many years ago."

¹Praise the LORD.
Praise God in his sanctuary;
    praise him in his mighty heavens.
²Praise him for his acts of power;
    praise him for his surpassing greatness.
³Praise him with the sounding of the trumpet,
    praise him with the harp and lyre,
⁴praise him with timbrel and dancing,
    praise him with the strings and pipe,
⁵praise him with the clash of cymbals,
    praise him with resounding cymbals.
⁶Let everything that has breath praise the LORD.
Praise the LORD.

PSALM 150

WAVES OF PRAISE

31

*Let everything that has breath
praise the LORD.
Praise the LORD.*
PSALM 150:6

"The complexities of the natural world amaze me, Lord. Sometimes, however, I get all caught up in what they do for me, and I pay no attention to what they tell me about you. I am amazed, for example, that a slight but steady wind can stir up such strong waves on Lake Michigan. The surging waters provide an exhilarating ride, but they also ought to remind me of something about you: your transcendence above nature. I am also intrigued that the breath of one human can call me to attention with a single trumpet blast or put me to sleep with the lullabye of a flute. The sounds of music can both energize and relax me, but they also ought to remind me of your immanence in creation. May I not just ride the waves of excitement and coast on the enjoyable sounds of music when I worship you. May I add the sound of my voice in speaking truth in song on Sunday and the movement of my body in doing good as I worship you throughout the week. And may even the faintest breath of praise in our church sanctuary and in our lives contribute to the current that will create waves of praise around the world forevermore."

¹Listen to my words, LORD,
   consider my lament.
²Hear my cry for help,
   my King and my God,
   for to you I pray.
³In the morning LORD, you hear my voice;
   in the morning I lay my requests before you
   and wait expectantly.
⁴For you are not a God who is pleased with wickedness;
   with you, evil people are not welcome.
⁵The arrogant cannot stand
   in your presence.

¹¹But let all who take refuge in you be glad;
   let them ever sing for joy.
Spread your protection over them,
   that those who love your name may rejoice in you.
¹²Surely, LORD, you bless the righteous;
   you surround them with your favor as with a shield.

PSALM 5:1–5, 11–12

LIFE ISN'T FAIR, LORD

32

Listen to my words, LORD, consider
my lament. Hear my cry for help,
my King and my God, for to you I pray.
PSALM 5:1–2

"Life isn't fair, Lord. I've been proclaiming this since childhood, as if this knowledge would help me unlock the secrets of the universe. But this is not news to you. You've been watching death, disease, and disaster wreak havoc on creation ever since Eve fell for Satan's lie. Why is it, though, that when trouble comes I run from rather than toward you? Is it because fragments of truth were left in human consciousness after the Fall and one of the sharpest pieces is from the truth that sickness and sorrow were never meant to be? Is it because I keep trying to force this pointed piece into the wrong place, blaming you for allowing evil rather than praising you for creating so much good? Thank you, Lord, for making a place for our questions, for letting us know that it is better to be like Job, who went to you when he couldn't understand evil, than like Eve, who entertained Satan because she thought she knew what was good. And it's better to be like the disciples, who admitted they had questions, than like the Pharisees, who claimed they had answers. When sickness and sorrow come, keep us from looking back and offering theories as to what went wrong; instead, keep us looking ahead and asking you how it can be made right. Focus our attention on the kingdom you are creating rather than on the one Satan is destroying. Accept our worship as an expression of faith in what is to come—a day when all creation will sing 'Alleluia to our God and King.'"

^{1}I will give thanks to you, LORD, with all my heart;
   I will tell of all your wonderful deeds.
^{2}I will be glad and rejoice in you;
   I will sing the praises of your name, O Most High.

^{7}The LORD reigns forever;
   he has established his throne for judgment.
^{8}He rules the world in righteousness
   and judges the peoples with equity.
^{9}The LORD is a refuge for the oppressed,
   a stronghold in times of trouble.
^{10}Those who know your name trust in you,
   for you, LORD, have never forsaken those who seek
         you.
^{11}Sing the praises of the LORD, enthroned in Zion;
   proclaim among the nations what he has done.

PSALM 9:1–2, 7–11

THANK YOU FOR YOUR PATIENCE WITH ME

33

I will give thanks to you, LORD, with all my heart;
I will tell of all your wonderful deeds.
I will be glad and rejoice in you;
I will sing the praises of your name, O Most High.
PSALM 9:1–2

"As I take the time to consider all the wonders you have accomplished without my help, Lord, I am amazed that you would seemingly burden yourself by getting involved with me. Certainly your work on earth has slowed down considerably since you created human beings. What a risk you took, Father, in letting me call myself by your name. How often I have been an embarrassment to you rather than a joy. I rush to defend myself when you want me to trust you. I love justice only when I am being treated unjustly, not when I am behaving unjustly. I claim to be righteous when you want me to confess my unrighteousness. I am realizing that much of the help I give you only slows you down. Thank you for your patience with me. May I learn that my task is not to bring in your kingdom; it is to purify myself with your help as I await the time when you usher me into glory. For whatever success you give me in this task, I will be sure to give you the glory and all the praise."

¹Praise the LORD.
Sing to the LORD a new song,
   his praise in the assembly of his faithful people.

⁴For the LORD takes delight in his people;
   he crowns the humble with victory.
⁵Let his faithful people rejoice in this honor
   and sing for joy on their beds.

PSALM 149:1, 4–5

¹Praise the LORD.
Praise God in his sanctuary;
   praise him in his mighty heavens.
²Praise him for his acts of power;
   praise him for his surpassing greatness.

⁶Let everything that has breath praise the LORD.
   Praise the LORD.

PSALM 150:1–2, 6

RECONCILED

For the LORD takes delight in his people;
he crowns the humble with victory.
PSALM 149:4

"Thank you, Lord, that you are the beginning and the end of all things—the Alpha and the Omega, the God of the new as well as the old, the God of what was as well as what is yet to be. Forgive me for thinking that I can judge everything that happens from my finite position in this present moment. Thank you that I am tucked safely in between the past and the future where I can have the assurance that every ending is also a new beginning and that even unhappy beginnings can have joyous endings. I read in the book of Esther what happened to evil Haman—who found happiness in exalting himself before the king while scheming to kill others. I noticed the contrast to humble Esther—who found joy after humbling herself before the king while risking her life to save others. Forgive me for thinking like Haman, whose happiness was rooted in pride and hatred. May I instead make it my goal each day to be reconciled to you through repentance and then to others through confession and forgiveness. May we all as followers of Jesus be reconciled to you and one another so we can then participate with you in reconciling others to yourself. May I begin each day with a prayer of praise for who you are and end it with a song of exaltation for what you have done and will do. For you are the Lord of heaven and Lord of my life! And joy comes only in proclaiming your name and praising your greatness. Praise the Lord!"

¹Have mercy on me, my God, have mercy on me,
   for in you I take refuge.
I will take refuge in the shadow of your wings
   until the disaster has passed.

⁵Be exalted, O God, above the heavens;
   let your glory be over all the earth.

⁷My heart, O God, is steadfast,
   my heart is steadfast;
   I will sing and make music.
⁸Awake, my soul!
   Awake, harp and lyre!
   I will awaken the dawn.
⁹I will praise you, Lord, among the nations;
   I will sing of you among the peoples.
¹⁰For great is your love, reaching to the heavens;
   your faithfulness reaches to the skies.
¹¹Be exalted, O God, above the heavens;
   let your glory be over all the earth.

PSALM 57:1, 5, 7–11

Taking Little Notice

35

Have mercy on me, my God,
have mercy on me, for in you I take refuge.
I will take refuge in the shadow of your wings
until the disaster has passed.
PSALM 57:1

"Why is it, Lord, that I learn the most when life takes a turn for the worst? Your servant David discovered this when he was hiding in a cave from King Saul. Chinese pastors realize it when they call prison a seminary. And we all come to understand it sooner or later when life breaks down and we simply cannot fix it. Why is it, Lord, that I learn so little when you give me your best? I know the world is broken, but I pay little attention because life for me is good. I know that people around the world are being persecuted for proclaiming truth, but I take little notice because I am guaranteed freedom of speech. May I not wait until my freedom is gone to decide to use it. May I not be ashamed to say that I love you."

¹God presides in the great assembly;
  he renders judgment among the "gods":
²"How long will you defend the unjust
  and show partiality to the wicked?
³Defend the weak and the fatherless;
  uphold the cause of the poor and the oppressed.
⁴Rescue the weak and the needy;
  deliver them from the hand of the wicked.
⁵"The 'gods' know nothing, they understand nothing.
  They walk about in darkness;
  all the foundations of the earth are shaken.
⁶"I said, 'You are "gods";
  you are all sons of the Most High.'
⁷But you will die like mere mortals;
  you will fall like every other ruler."
⁸Rise up, O God, judge the earth,
  for all the nations are your inheritance.

PSALM 82

JOINING WITH JESUS

36

Defend the weak and the fatherless;
uphold the cause of the poor and the oppressed.
Rescue the weak and the needy;
deliver them from the hand of the wicked.
PSALM 82:3–4

"The kings of this earth are at war again, Lord. So what's new? People fighting so they can live in peace, or so the story goes. Yeah, right! People fighting so they can be in power is more like it. Not much has changed in the last twenty centuries. Everyone loves freedom. Everyone hates oppression. Lord Jesus, two thousand years ago, the Jews thought you were going to rally the troops and lead them to freedom from Rome, just as Moses had delivered them from the Egyptians and King David had led them to defeat the Philistines. But you had a surprise for them. You were introducing a new strategy: A kingdom of love and light instead of power and might. This was not a popular idea then, and it's not one that gets a lot of votes today. It's a lot easier to fight the enemy who oppresses our bodies than the one who is trying to rule our hearts. May I join you today, Lord, in going to war against the evil in my own heart—jealousy, greed, pride, and hatred—so your kingdom of peace may come, so your will may be done on earth as it is in heaven."

¹I love the LORD, for he heard my voice;
   he heard my cry for mercy.
²Because he turned his ear to me,
   I will call on him as long as I live.
³The cords of death entangled me,
   the anguish of the grave came over me;
   I was overcome by distress and sorrow.
⁴Then I called on the name of the LORD:
   "LORD, save me!"

¹²What shall I return to the LORD
   for all his goodness to me?
¹³I will lift up the cup of salvation
   and call on the name of the LORD.
¹⁴I will fulfill my vows to the LORD
   in the presence of all his people.
¹⁵Precious in the sight of the LORD
   is the death of his faithful servants.

¹⁹in the courts of the house of the LORD—
   in your midst, Jerusalem.
Praise the LORD.

PSALM 116:1–4, 12–15, 19

A WORD ABOUT DEATH

37

The cords of death entangled me, the anguish
of the grave came over me; I was overcome
by distress and sorrow. Then I called on the name
of the LORD: "LORD, save me!"
PSALM 116:3–4

"Death is all around us, Lord. Death of dreams, death of relationships, death of loved ones. We call death painful; you call it precious. We see it as the end; you see it as the beginning. We consider it loss; you count it gain. Our vision is too limited to see any good in it. So, in our eagerness to prevent something bad from happening, we get in the way of the good you want to do. In our attempts to protect what we think is right, we thwart your plan to expose what you know is wrong. In using our power to keep what we love from dying, we keep ourselves from witnessing your resurrection power. Often in church I sing, 'Forever I'll love you, forever I'll stand,' but, like Peter did in the days of your trial, before Monday morning I will fail to keep that promise. Fear still causes me to believe that losing my way of life is worse than losing my soul. Thank you, Lord, that you didn't let the fear of death keep you from winning everlasting life for me. Thank you that when the forces of hell threaten to overtake me, I don't have to stay ahead of them. I only have to stay with you, for you keep Satan in his place. And his place is always behind you. Praise the Lord."

¹Ascribe to the LORD, you heavenly beings,
    ascribe to the LORD glory and strength.
²Ascribe to the LORD the glory due his name;
    worship the LORD in the splendor of his holiness.
³The voice of the LORD is over the waters;
    the God of glory thunders,
    the LORD thunders over the mighty waters.
⁴The voice of the LORD is powerful;
    the voice of the LORD is majestic.

⁹The voice of the LORD twists the oaks
    and strips the forests bare.
And in his temple all cry, "Glory!"
¹⁰The LORD sits enthroned over the flood;
    the LORD is enthroned as King forever.
¹¹The LORD gives strength to his people;
    the LORD blesses his people with peace.

PSALM 29:1–4, 9–11

A Ballet of Birds

38

The voice of the LORD is over the waters;
the God of glory thunders,
the LORD thunders over the mighty waters.
PSALM 29:3

"Straight ahead of me, against a clear blue sky, a small gray cloud hovered above the highway. *What was that lonely cloud doing there on such a perfect Sunday afternoon?* I wondered as I headed for a choir rehearsal at church. Almost as if it heard my thoughts, the cloud suddenly shimmered like silver and disappeared. Then just as suddenly it reappeared, darker this time, and in a new shape. A smile. And then the cloud stretched itself across the road like a wavy banner announcing the song my favorite radio station was playing. As the music of 'This Is My Father's World' beamed from distant radio towers, the cloud of birds swelled and soared with each majestic phrase, then dipped and danced with each dramatic beat. They didn't know it, but the station was playing 'their song.' Thank you, Lord, for allowing me to watch you conduct such a remarkable ballet of birds. Thank you for reminding me that all creation, myself included, is your song and that you are conducting every single verse. Thank you, Father, that this is indeed your world and that you have already won the battle over sin and sickness, the devil and death. May our sacrifice of praise each time we gather to glorify you in song be as beautiful to you as your gift of creation is to us."

⁵Then I acknowledged my sin to you
   and did not cover up my iniquity.
I said, "I will confess
   my transgressions to the LORD."
And you forgave
   the guilt of my sin.
⁶Therefore let all the faithful pray to you
   while you may be found;
surely the rising of the mighty waters
   will not reach them.
⁷You are my hiding place;
   you will protect me from trouble
   and surround me with songs of deliverance.
⁸I will instruct you and teach you in the way you should go;
   I will counsel you with my loving eye on you.
⁹Do not be like the horse or the mule,
   which have no understanding
but must be controlled by bit and bridle
   or they will not come to you.
¹⁰Many are the woes of the wicked,
   but the LORD's unfailing love
   surrounds the one who trusts in him.
¹¹Rejoice in the LORD and be glad, you righteous;
   sing, all you who are upright in heart!

PSALM 32:5–11

Body and Spirit: The Odd Couple

39

Then I acknowledged my sin to you
and did not cover up my iniquity.
I said, "I will confess my transgressions to the LORD."
PSALM 32:5

"When will I understand, Lord, that the thing that gives me the most comfort may be the very thing that condemns me? When will I realize that the thing that most terrifies me is the only thing that can save me? I find comfort in my own efforts, but I know that all my straining for safety only feeds the illusion that I am in control. The thing that most terrifies me is you, Lord, for you insist that I relinquish control. This idea is not an easy one for me to sell to my body and spirit, who already have a hard time getting along. What my body claims to 'need' conflicts with what my spirit says is good, and what my spirit says is good my body cannot do. They are like the original odd couple. So here I am, straining to hold them together, often hopelessly forgetting that your love has already accomplished the task while still sadly trusting my work rather than yours. Thank you, Lord, that the only righteousness I need comes from you and begins in my heart through honest confession and heartfelt praise. Amen."

¹Sing joyfully to the LORD, you righteous;
    it is fitting for the upright to praise him.

³Sing to him a new song;
    play skillfully, and shout for joy.
⁴For the word of the LORD is right and true;
    he is faithful in all he does.

⁶By the word of the LORD the heavens were made,
    their starry host by the breath of his mouth.

⁸Let all the earth fear the LORD;
    let all the people of the world revere him.
⁹For he spoke, and it came to be;
    he commanded, and it stood firm.
¹⁰The LORD foils the plans of the nations;
    he thwarts the purposes of the peoples.
¹¹But the plans of the LORD stand firm forever,
    the purposes of his heart through all generations.

²¹In him our hearts rejoice,
    for we trust in his holy name.
²²May your unfailing love be with us, LORD,
    even as we put our hope in you.

PSALM 33:1, 3–4, 6, 8–11, 21–22

EMPTYING THE TRASH

In him our hearts rejoice,
for we trust in his holy name.
PSALM 33:21

"For many years, Father, I have called myself by your name, but too often I have used the relationship to benefit myself rather than others. Even though I acknowledge that you are Lord, I still try to get my way. I still think life would be better if people would move when I am restless and stop when I need rest. I still think the reason I can't get my life cleaned up is because others keep messing it up. I still think the garbage I smell belongs to someone else. I should know better, though, for you say that it's not what's outside of me that contaminates me, but what's inside. The real garbage is all those thoughts and attitudes that cause me to turn up my nose at a tiny whiff of someone else's sin while ignoring the stench of my own. Forgive me for refusing to empty my trash, Lord. And may I lose all desire to keep it when I see what damage it does to your awesome creation."

¹We have heard it with our ears, O God;
  our ancestors have told us
what you did in their days,
  in days long ago.
²With your hand you drove out the nations
  and planted our ancestors;
you crushed the peoples
  and made our ancestors flourish.
³It was not by their sword that they won the land,
  nor did their arm bring them victory;
it was your right hand, your arm,
  and the light of your face, for you loved them.
⁴You are my King and my God,
  who decrees victories for Jacob.
⁵Through you we push back our enemies;
  through your name we trample our foes.
⁶I put no trust in my bow,
  my sword does not bring me victory;
⁷but you give us victory over our enemies,
  you put our adversaries to shame.
⁸In God we make our boast all day long,
  and we will praise your name forever.

PSALM 44:1–8

BEHIND THE SCENES

But you give us victory over our enemies,
you put our adversaries to shame.
PSALM 44:7

"Thank you, Lord, that the forces of evil taking cen-
ter stage in this world are only a small part of the real
drama. Forgive me for judging the entire performance by
one short scene. And forgive me for judging the whole
play by my small role. Thank you for the past, which
shows me the work you have done; for the present, which
gives me a chance to participate in the work you are still
doing; and for the future, which will reveal the work you
have accomplished. When I become discouraged about
the evil that is so visible, remind me of the heavenly forces
working behind the scenes to bring about your plan for
the ages. May our praise always be a foretaste of what is
to come when human voices join the chorus of angels in
an everlasting worship celebration of your final victory
over evil."

¹²People, despite their wealth, do not endure;
  they are like the beasts that perish.
¹³This is the fate of those who trust in themselves,
  and of their followers, who approve their sayings.

¹⁶Do not be overawed when others grow rich,
  when the splendor of their houses increases;
¹⁷for they will take nothing with them when they die,
  their splendor will not descend with them.
¹⁸Though while they live they count themselves
    blessed—
  and people praise you when you prosper—
¹⁹they will join those who have gone before them,
  who will never again see the light of life.
²⁰People who have wealth but lack understanding
  are like the beasts that perish.

PSALM 49:12–13, 16–20

MULTIPLY YOUR GOODNESS

Do not be overawed when others grow rich,
when the splendor of their houses increases;
for they will take nothing with them when they die.
PSALM 49:16–17

"Why is it, Lord, that I compare myself only to those who have more rather than to those who have less? Why is it so difficult for me to understand that when you write about rich people you mean me, not those who make a higher salary or live in a bigger house? And why do my comparisons always involve physical blessings like wealth and comfort rather than spiritual blessings like truth and love, grace, and mercy? Lord, why is it so difficult for me to comprehend the treasure I have in knowing you and experiencing your forgiveness? Why do I keep these things to myself as if there's not enough to go around? Why can I not be as generous to others as you have been to me? Dear Father, I thank you for my riches—both physical and spiritual—but I plead for understanding as well so I won't hoard your goodness like an animal concerned only with its own survival. Increase our understanding, O God, so we might multiply your goodness wherever life's journey takes us. May the joy of knowing you spread across all the earth as a result of our worship."

¹Be merciful to me, my God,
　　for my enemies are in hot pursuit;
　　all day long they press their attack.
²My adversaries pursue me all day long;
　　in their pride many are attacking me.
³When I am afraid, I put my trust in you.

⁸Record my misery;
　　list my tears on your scroll—
　　are they not in your record?
⁹Then my enemies will turn back
　　when I call for help.
　　By this I will know that God is for me.
¹⁰In God, whose word I praise,
　　in the LORD, whose word I praise—
¹¹in God I trust and am not afraid.
　　What can man do to me?

¹³For you have delivered me from death
　　and my feet from stumbling,
that I may walk before God
　　in the light of life.

PSALM 56:1–3, 8–11, 13

THE HAPPY REUNION OF TRUTH AND MERCY

Be merciful to me, my God.
PSALM 56:1

"Thank you for my senses, Lord. They serve me well in the physical world by enabling me to enjoy its pleasures and avoid its dangers. In regard to the spiritual world, however, they often deceive me. Although they are quick to reveal what is wrong with everyone else, they lie about what is wrong with me. My eyes tell me when someone else is immodest, but they don't tell me when I am envious. My ears tell me when someone slanders me, but they don't tell me when I use truth to deceive. My skin tells me when the room is the wrong temperature, but it doesn't tell me when my heart is cold and arrogant or hot and foolish. If I am to know these things, Lord, you must reveal them. Long ago you formed me out of dust and later gave me spiritual life by adding living water.* Today I need a mixture of dust and water applied to my eyes like you once did for a blind man, so I will be able to see spiritually as well as I do physically. May I not hide in the darkness of sin but walk in the shining light of your love. Help me not to miss the happy reunion of truth and mercy."

---

*John 7:38

¹Have mercy on me, my God, have mercy on me,
   for in you I take refuge.
I will take refuge in the shadow of your wings
   until the disaster has passed.
²I cry out to God Most High,
   to God, who vindicates me.
³He sends from heaven and saves me,
   rebuking those who hotly pursue me—
God sends forth his love and his faithfulness.

⁹I will praise you, Lord, among the nations;
   I will sing of you among the peoples.
¹⁰For great is your love, reaching to the heavens;
   your faithfulness reaches to the skies.
¹¹Be exalted, O God, above the heavens;
   let your glory be over all the earth.

PSALM 57:1–3, 9–11

Turning Our Hearts Toward You

Have mercy on me, my God,
have mercy on me,
for in you I take refuge.
I will take refuge in the shadow
of your wings until the disaster has passed.
PSALM 57:1

"Thank you, Lord, that your plan for all of creation is to make your glory cover all of the earth. Thank you for choosing us to be your partners in this marvelous undertaking by allowing us to wear the glorious garments of your righteousness. Thank you for new beginnings that depend not on clocks and calendars but on the cross. Thank you for recent reminders of the hope that change can bring. But turning the page of history is of little significance compared to the daily act of turning our hearts toward you. I confess that I often spend more time pouting about my circumstances than shouting about your power to use them for good. As I turn my heart toward you today, change the hurt of crushing circumstances into the wine of godly blessing that will bring joy and healing to others. Change my failure and brokenness into bread that will feed the spiritually hungry so they too will know that nothing compares to the promise we have in you."

⁵ Yes, my soul, find rest in God;
    my hope comes from him.
⁶ Truly he is my rock and my salvation;
    he is my fortress, I will not be shaken.
⁷ My salvation and my honor depend on God;
    he is my mighty rock, my refuge.
⁸ Trust in him at all times, you people;
    pour out your hearts to him,
    for God is our refuge.

¹¹ One thing God has spoken,
    two things I have heard:
"Power belongs to you, God,
    ¹² and with you, Lord, is unfailing love";
and, "You reward everyone
    according to what they have done."

PSALM 62:5–8, 11–12

THE GREATNESS AND GOODNESS OF GOD

*"Power belongs to you, God,
and with you, Lord, is unfailing love."*
PSALM 62:11

" 'God is great, God is good.' The words are so familiar that we read them without thinking—without realizing the profound truth they hold. For without your greatness, Lord, the universe would be like a junkyard of banged up stars and planets. And without your goodness, Father, the earth would be like a playground ruled by the biggest bully. Thank you for using your greatness to save me rather than to destroy me. Thank you for using your goodness as a way to reach me rather than as a reason to reject me. Keep me from believing that I need something more complex than your simple truth. And keep me from thinking that I can find anything more satisfying than your selfless love."

²I have seen you in the sanctuary
and beheld your power and your glory.
³Because your love is better than life,
my lips will glorify you.
⁴I will praise you as long as I live,
and in your name I will lift up my hands.

⁷Because you are my help,
I sing in the shadow of your wings.
⁸I cling to you;
Your right hand upholds me.

PSALM 63:2–4, 7–8

⁹All people will fear;
they will proclaim the works of God
and ponder what he has done.
¹⁰The righteous will rejoice in the LORD
and take refuge in him;
all the upright in heart will glory in him!

PSALM 64:9–10

A Celebration of Love

Your love is better than life.
PSALM 63:3

"Each year, Lord, we set aside a special day for a celebration of love. Valentine's Day, we call it, but you already knew that. We send cards with pretty pictures, and we renew our promises with flowery words. But in reality, we know so little about love, Lord. We have redefined the one word that best describes your character and have removed all of its sacred meaning. We have been so bombarded with the world's definition that we have forgotten yours. You say that love is patient, kind, does not envy, does not boast, is not rude, self-seeking, or easily angered, keeps no record of wrongs, always protects, trusts, hopes, and perseveres, never fails.* You even say that love lays down its life.** Lovers today believe they shouldn't have to give up anything for one another, much less their lives. Will we ever learn that 'your love is better than life, Lord?' Not until we turn off the life-support systems of this world and allow your heart to beat inside us. Then we will know that you alone are worthy to be praised."

*See 1 Corinthians 13
**See 1 John 3:16

¹³I will come to your temple with burnt offerings
and fulfill my vows to you—
¹⁴vows my lips promised and my mouth spoke
when I was in trouble.

¹⁶Come and hear, all you who fear God;
let me tell you what he has done for me.
¹⁷I cried out to him with my mouth;
his praise was on my tongue.
¹⁸If I had cherished sin in my heart,
the Lord would not have listened;
¹⁹but God has surely listened
and has heard my prayer.
²⁰Praise be to God,
who has not rejected my prayer
or withheld his love from me!

PSALM 66:13–14, 16–20

³⁵You, God, are awesome in your sanctuary;
the God of Israel gives power and strength to
his people.
Praise be to God!

PSALM 68:35

CHOCOLATE AND JESUS

47

Praise be to God, who has not rejected
my prayer or withheld his love from me!
PSALM 66:20

"Sometimes we celebrate human love with tasty chocolates and shiny red hearts, Lord. But your love is more than sweet and pretty; it's also deep and powerful. It doesn't just melt hearts; it explodes in power and praise. But our language is limited, and the only word I have to express this amazing truth is the same word I use to describe my craving for chocolate. Is it any surprise that we can't fully comprehend your love? I need a separate word, a unique word, a holy word to express the awesome wonder of it. Thank you, Father, that there is such a Word: It is Jesus, the Lover of my soul—the blessing promised to Abraham and the reason I can be a blessing. He is the One who rules heaven and reigns on earth as we—His people—give Him full reign in our hearts and lives."

¹May God be gracious to us and bless us
  and make his face shine on us—
²so that your ways may be known on earth,
  your salvation among all nations.
³May the peoples praise you, God;
  may all the peoples praise you.
⁴May the nations be glad and sing for joy,
  for you rule the peoples with equity
  and guide the nations of the earth.
⁵May the peoples praise you, God;
  may all the peoples praise you.
⁶The land yields its harvest;
  God, our God, blesses us.
⁷May God bless us still,
  so that all the ends of the earth will fear him.

PSALM 67

A Sacred Covenant

*May God be gracious to us and bless us
and make his face shine on us—
so that your ways may be known on earth,
your salvation among all nations.*
PSALM 67:1–2

"Regarding marriage, Lord, I have trouble remembering that it is more than just a physical and emotional relationship designed for my comfort and pleasure; it is also a spiritual relationship designed to show the world how you relate to your people. Elevate my thinking about this sacred covenant. Remind me that I am participating in a holy relationship you designed as a way to bless all creation. You have indeed done great things for those of us who are married, Lord, and we know that you also want to do great things through us. Display your compassion in us as spouses so all the world will see it. And let your love continually flow through us so that one day soon all heaven and earth will join us in blessing your holy name."

¹⁴ As for me, I will always have hope;
  I will praise you more and more.
¹⁵ My mouth will tell of your righteous deeds,
  of your saving acts all day long—
  though I know not how to relate them all.
¹⁶ I will come and proclaim your mighty acts,
    Sovereign LORD;
  I will proclaim your righteous deeds, yours alone.
¹⁷ Since my youth, God, you have taught me,
  and to this day I declare your marvelous deeds.
¹⁸ Even when I am old and gray,
  do not forsake me, my God,
till I declare your power to the next generation,
  your mighty acts to all who are to come.

²² I will praise you with the harp
  for your faithfulness, my God;
I will sing praise to you with the lyre,
  Holy One of Israel.
²³ My lips will shout for joy
  when I sing praise to you—
  I whom you have delivered.

PSALM 71:14–18, 22–23

A Focus on Beauty

I will come and proclaim
your mighty acts, Sovereign LORD;
I will proclaim your righteous deeds,
yours alone.
PSALM 71:16

"I admit, Lord, that I find it easy, even enjoyable, to point out everything I see that is wrong with the world. However, that is not what the world needs or what you want. Anyone with eyes can see what is wrong, but only those who listen to you will have the wisdom to show the world how to make it right. The world needs to see the change you have made in my life, not hear me grumble about the changes I want others to make in theirs. And you want people who are recognized for the praise they raise, not for the condemnation they lower. I know, Lord, that your faithfulness is to all generations, not just my own. And I know that your mercy is for everyone, not just me. Help me to focus on the good you are doing rather than on the evil others seem to be getting away with. When we do, the beauty of our lives will call people of all ages to worship you, and the beauty of our worship will call all generations to live holy lives."

^{19}Your righteousness, God, reaches to the heavens,
you who have done great things.
Who is like you, God?

^{22}I will praise you with the harp
for your faithfulness, my God;
I will sing praise to you with the lyre,
Holy One of Israel.
^{23}My lips will shout for joy
when I sing praise to you—
I whom you have delivered.
^{24}My tongue will tell of your righteous acts
all day long,
for those who wanted to harm me
have been put to shame and confusion.

PSALM 71:19, 22–24

THE FRAGILE ROSEBUD 50

My lips will shout for joy
when I sing praise to you.
PSALM 71:23

"I'm sure you recall, Lord of my life, when a pale pink rosebud caught my attention, and I knelt to inhale its sweet fragrance. Reaching around the thorns, I touched the tip of the fragile flower. Then, as I watched in silent wonder, the petals unfolded before me, and the tight little bud became a full-flowered rose. Since then I have touched many rosebuds hoping for a repeat performance, but nothing like that has ever happened again. The nation of Israel during the time of Moses was much like that fragile rosebud from my childhood. Then you knelt down, O God of Israel, and touched it—causing it to unfold into a fragrant and beautiful display of your glory. We too are waiting for your touch, Lord, so your stunning glory can be displayed in our lives. Today we want our hearts to unfold like flowers before you, open to your Son of love."

¹⁰May the kings of Tarshish and of distant shores
  bring tribute to him.
May the kings of Sheba and Seba
  present him gifts.
¹¹May all kings bow down to him
  and all nations serve him.
¹²For he will deliver the needy who cry out,
  the afflicted who have no one to help.
¹³He will take pity on the weak and the needy
  and save the needy from death.
¹⁴He will rescue them from oppression and violence,
  for precious is their blood in his sight.

¹⁷May his name endure forever;
  may it continue as long as the sun.
Then all nations will be blessed through him,
  and they will call him blessed.
¹⁸Praise be to the LORD God, the God of Israel,
  who alone does marvelous deeds.
¹⁹Praise be to his glorious name forever;
  may the whole earth be filled with his glory.
Amen and Amen.

PSALM 72:10–14, 17–19
A PSALM ABOUT SOLOMON

A QUEST FOR WISDOM

51

Praise be to the LORD God, the God of Israel,
who alone does marvelous deeds.
PSALM 72:18

"Lord, there's a lesson I need to learn about wisdom, but I don't know what it is. I know I need it, and I know you want me to have it, but I seem to have a short supply. You rewarded Solomon with wealth because he asked for wisdom to rule justly. Am I lacking wisdom because I want it for the wrong reason? After hearing about Solomon's great wisdom, the queen of Sheba went to see for herself. By the time she left, though, she wasn't praising Solomon; she was praising you for loving your people so much that you gave them a ruler who used wisdom to maintain justice and righteousness. I confess, Lord, that I sometimes behave as if my mind is my personal playground and that I have the right to entertain whatever thoughts give me pleasure. Forgive me for this foolish thinking and grant me the kind of wisdom that keeps justice and righteousness alive, that looks out for the needy and oppressed, and that causes people to worship you. In other words, give me the same mind you gave Christ, for I know I will not be fit to rule in heaven if I don't learn how to rule on earth."

¹I cried out to God for help;
  I cried out to God to hear me.
²When I was in distress, I sought the Lord;
  at night I stretched out untiring hands,
  and I would not be comforted.

⁷"Will the Lord reject forever?
  Will he never show his favor again?
⁸Has his unfailing love vanished forever?
  Has his promise failed for all time?
⁹Has God forgotten to be merciful?
  Has he in anger withheld his compassion?"
¹⁰Then I thought, "To this I will appeal:
  the years when the Most High stretched out
      his right hand.
¹¹I will remember the deeds of the LORD;
  yes, I will remember your miracles of long ago.
¹²I will consider all your works
  and meditate on all your mighty deeds."
¹³Your ways, God, are holy.
  What god is as great as our God?
¹⁴You are the God who performs miracles;
  you display your power among the peoples.

PSALM 77:1–2, 7–14

"It All Makes Me Think"

52

Your ways, God, are holy.
What god is as great as our God?
You are the God who performs miracles;
you display your power among the peoples.
PSALM 77:13–14

"All the hatred I see in this world makes me question your love, Lord. All the suffering makes me think you're unfair. Sometimes your slowness makes me think you're too busy. And sometimes your silence makes me think you don't care. I like talking about faith, Lord, but I prefer hiding behind doubt. I like the idea of waiting on you, but usually I'm too busy to notice when you stop. I like saying that I follow you, but I'd rather step into your shoes than out of my own. I like being assured of your love, but I feel safer in my traditions. I like the idea of peace, but I'm afraid to give up my anger. I like singing about your strength, but I'd rather have people think it belongs to me. I like it when you display your power to me. May I also be willing to have you display your power through me."

¹My people, hear my teaching;
   listen to the words of my mouth.
²I will open my mouth with a parable;
   I will utter hidden things, things from of old—
³things we have heard and known,
   things our ancestors have told us.
⁴We will not hide them from their descendants;
   we will tell the next generation
the praiseworthy deeds of the LORD,
   his power, and the wonders he has done.
⁵He decreed statutes for Jacob
   and established the law in Israel,
which he commanded our ancestors
   to teach their children,
⁶so the next generation would know them,
   even the children yet to be born,
   and they in turn would tell their children.
⁷Then they would put their trust in God
   and would not forget his deeds
   but would keep his commands.

PSALM 78:1–7

ONLY YOU

53

We will tell the next generation
the praiseworthy deeds of the LORD, his power,
and the wonders he has done.
PSALM 78:4

"Some people say that more knowledge will save civilization from extinction; some say that stricter law enforcement will protect citizens from evil; others say that more human kindness will put an end to all suffering. But better education can't change desires, stronger laws can't improve behavior, and more compassion can't eliminate hatred. And all of that is true of me as well, Lord. More knowledge about you won't save me, more self-discipline won't get me into your kingdom, and more acts of compassion won't turn my heart or anyone else's toward you. Only you can do any of those things. We worship you because that is indeed what you want to do for us, in us, and through us. Make our knowledge holy and our motives pure. May we be wholly devoted to you."

⁵²But he brought his people out like a flock;
   he led them like sheep through the
          wilderness.

⁷⁰He chose David his servant
   and took him from the sheep pens;
⁷¹from tending the sheep he brought him
   to be the shepherd of his people Jacob,
   of Israel his inheritance.
⁷²And David shepherded them with integrity of heart;
   with skillful hands he led them.

PSALM 78:52, 70–72

¹³Then we your people, the sheep of your pasture,
   will praise you forever;
from generation to generation
   we will proclaim your praise.

PSALM 79:13

¹Hear us, Shepherd of Israel,
   you who lead Joseph like a flock.
You who sit enthroned between the cherubim,
   shine forth
²before Ephraim, Benjamin and Manasseh.
   Awaken your might;
   come and save us.
³Restore us, O God;
   make your face shine on us,
   that we may be saved.

PSALM 80:1–3

WHEN THE SHEPHERD LEADS

Hear us, Shepherd of Israel,
you who lead Joseph like a flock.
PSALM 80:1

"Thank you, Lord, that you lead us like sheep to green pastures rather than herding us like cattle to the slaughterhouse. Thank you that when you lead, no one is trampled in a stampede. Thank you for allowing me to live in a nation that promises me the right to pursue happiness. But keep reminding me that it is only in pursuing you that I will find joy. When I pursue my own happiness alone, I make others miserable by using them to fill my need. But when I pursue you, I am able to meet the needs of others because I am filled with your joy. Show us the light of your face, Lord, so we can follow you. Fill us with the light of your love so we can help others find you. May our joyful adoration of you lead us into your glorious presence and give us a taste of eternal gladness."

¹Sing for joy to God our strength;
  shout aloud to the God of Jacob!
²Begin the music, strike the timbrel,
  play the melodious harp and lyre.

⁷In your distress you called and I rescued you,
  I answered you out of a thundercloud;
  I tested you at the waters of Meribah.
⁸Hear me, my people, and I will warn you—
  if you would only listen to me, Israel!
⁹You shall have no foreign god among you;
  you shall not worship any god other than me.
¹⁰I am the LORD your God,
  who brought you up out of Egypt.
Open wide your mouth and I will fill it.

PSALM 81:1–2, 7–10

OPEN MY EYES, EARS, AND HEART

55

*Sing for joy to God our strength;
shout aloud to the God of Jacob!*
PSALM 81:1

"Thank you, Lord, that you didn't stop choosing people after you made a nation out of Israel. Thank you that you didn't stop calling people after you made a church out of your disciples. Thank you that you didn't stop working in people's lives after you finished writing your best-selling book. Thank you that you're still willing and waiting to do your work through me. Sometimes I grumble that you are silent, but I know it's because I don't like what you're saying. Sometimes I complain that I can't see you, but I know it's because I don't want to believe the truth you're revealing. Sometimes I feel empty, but I know it's because I've been doing more grazing at the buffet table of popular culture than eating the simple but satisfying Bread of Life. Sometimes I feel lethargic and complacent, but I know it's because I've been consuming artificially sweetened ideas about life and love instead of the energizing and life-giving wine of your Spirit. Open my eyes, Lord, to see the work you are still doing in the world. Open my ears to hear the words you are speaking through singing and preaching. Open my heart to answer your call to a life of quiet strength, peaceful surrender, and great adventure."

¹Give praise to the LORD, proclaim his name;
    make known among the nations what he has done.
²Sing to him, sing praise to him;
    tell of all his wonderful acts.
³Glory in his holy name;
    let the hearts of those who seek the LORD rejoice.
⁴Look to the LORD and his strength;
    seek his face always.

⁷He is the LORD our God;
    his judgments are in all the earth.

PSALM 105:1–4, 7

¹³Then they cried to the LORD in their trouble,
    and he saved them from their distress.
¹⁴He brought them out of darkness, the utter darkness,
    and broke away their chains.
¹⁵Let them give thanks to the LORD for his unfailing
        love
    and his wonderful deeds for mankind,
¹⁶for he breaks down gates of bronze
    and cuts through bars of iron.

⁴³Let the one who is wise heed these things
    and ponder the loving deeds of the LORD.

PSALM 107:13–16, 43

The Trouble with Doubt

56

Give praise to the LORD, proclaim his name;
make known among the nations
what he has done. Sing to him, sing praise to him;
tell of all his wonderful acts.
PSALM 105:1–2

"Sometimes I live as if being 'converted' is the end of faith rather than just the beginning, Lord—as if being 'inside' the circle of belief means that I can go on with life as if nothing miraculous happened. Sometimes I still flirt with doubt because it offers me an excuse to lounge in my weakness rather than stand in your strength. Sometimes I forget that doubt is the prison where Satan makes people believe they have more freedom inside with him than outside with you. Forgive me for entertaining the idea that there is any freedom in sin. I know, Lord, that you didn't break down the bars that imprison me just so I could have a better view of the natural world; you did it so that I could walk through into the glorious expanse of your supernatural kingdom. I don't want to stop at the gates of your glory to admire it, Lord, I want to enter your presence and become part of it. Use me to glorify your name in all the earth."

[1]Hear me, Lord, and answer me,
    for I am poor and needy.
[2]Guard my life, for I am faithful to you;
    save your servant who trusts in you.
You are my God; [3]have mercy on me, Lord,
    for I call to you all day long.
[4]Bring joy to your servant, Lord,
    for I put my trust in you.
[5]You, Lord, are forgiving and good,
    abounding in love to all who call to you.
[6]Hear my prayer, Lord;
    listen to my cry for mercy.
[7]When I am in distress, I call to you,
    because you answer me.
[10]For you are great and do marvelous deeds;
    you alone are God.
[11]Teach me your way, Lord,
    that I may rely on your faithfulness;
give me an undivided heart,
    that I may fear your name.
[12]I will praise you, Lord my God, with all my heart;
    I will glorify your name forever.
[13]For great is your love toward me;
    you have delivered me from the depths,
    from the realm of the dead.

PSALM 86:1–7, 10–13

CELEBRATE RESURRECTION!

For great is your love toward me;
you have delivered me from the depths,
from the realm of the dead.
PSALM 86:13

57

"Resurrection. Such a common word with such uncommon meaning. I am here before you today to celebrate it, Lord, but I can't begin to comprehend it:

The creator of the universe becoming part of creation.

The giver of life giving himself over to death.

The one who is without sin bearing the weight of the whole world's sin.

The one whose home is heaven taking my place in hell.

The one who was dead overcoming death!

"Unprecedented. Hallelujah! I am no longer a slave to sin because you have overcome evil. Hallelujah! The grave will never hold me because you have defeated death! Hallelujah! I am forgiven because you have risen!"

¹⁴ "Because he loves me," says the LORD,
        "I will rescue him;
    I will protect him, for he acknowledges my name.
¹⁵ He will call on me, and I will answer him;
    I will be with him in trouble,
    I will deliver him and honor him.
¹⁶ With long life I will satisfy him
    and show him my salvation."

⁵ How great are your works, LORD,
    how profound your thoughts!
⁶ Senseless people do not know,
    fools do not understand,
⁷ that though the wicked spring up like grass
    and all evildoers flourish,
    they will be destroyed forever.
⁸ But you, LORD, are forever exalted.

PSALM 91:14–16; 92:5–8

A Difficult Prayer

How great are your works, LORD,
how profound your thoughts!
PSALM 92:5

"I do not want to pray this prayer, Jesus. It makes me sad and scared. Could you give me another one? I'm not saying it's a bad prayer. You prayed it, so it must be good. But the words get stuck in my throat. I'm sorry that after all these years of knowing you, I'm still afraid to say them. But I am. How did you bring yourself to say them when so much was at stake? Instead of asking for a few more years to finish the job you had started, you said, "It is finished." How did you have the courage to say it was finished when it looked as if you had failed? Instead of pleading for more time, you said, "Into your hands I commit my spirit." After doing the hardest part of the work, you trusted someone else to finish the job. Surely, that was something you learned in heaven, because we don't do things that way here on earth. I don't like saying, "It is finished" when I haven't yet won; I don't even like saying, "Into your hands I commit my plans." But if I can't say that, how can I say that I trust you with my spirit? So I'm asking today for courage to say, "It is finished." Just as you rested on the seventh day after creating the world, you "rested" on the seventh day after redeeming the world. By "resting" when it looked as if your work was not yet finished, you taught us that the only job well done is the one that God the Father completes. May I commit to you all of my plans and problems and enter the serenity of Sabbath rest."

¹Come, let us sing for joy to the LORD;
   let us shout aloud to the Rock of our salvation.
²Let us come before him with thanksgiving
   and extol him with music and song.
³For the LORD is the great God,
   the great King above all gods.

⁸"Do not harden your hearts as you did at Meribah,
   as you did that day at Massah in the wilderness."

PSALM 95:1–3, 8

THE SAVIOR WE NEEDED

59

For the LORD is the great God,
the great King above all gods.
PSALM 95:3

"I confess, Lord, that I allow my heart to be hardened when I don't get what I want from you. Like your children the Israelites, I want to be planted in the land of promise, not led through the desert of doubt. When the escapees from Egypt got to the Red Sea, they felt trapped. Looking ahead, they saw death by drowning; looking back they saw death by Pharaoh's army. But when they chose to die in obedience, they received life. When you were hanging on the cross, it looked as if you were trapped. To stay on the cross meant death for you; to come down would have meant death for us. But when you chose to die in obedience, we received life. Instead of saving yourself by coming down from the cross, you chose to save us by rising from the grave. Hallelujah! Thank you for becoming what the entire world needed—a Savior—rather than what one nation wanted—a king. We humbly acknowledge you as our risen Savior, and we joyfully anticipate the day when we will be able to crown you as our matchless King."

¹Sing to the LORD a new song,
    for he has done marvelous things;
his right hand and his holy arm
    have worked salvation for him.
²The LORD has made his salvation known
    and revealed his righteousness to the nations.
³He has remembered his love
    and his faithfulness to Israel;
all the ends of the earth have seen
    the salvation of our God.
⁴Shout for joy to the LORD, all the earth,
    burst into jubilant song with music;
⁵make music to the LORD with the harp,
    with the harp and the sound of singing,
⁶with trumpets and the blast of the ram's horn—
    shout for joy before the LORD, the King.
⁷Let the sea resound, and everything in it,
    the world, and all who live in it.
⁸Let the rivers clap their hands,
    let the mountains sing together for joy;
⁹let them sing before the LORD,
    for he comes to judge the earth.
He will judge the world in righteousness
    and the peoples with equity.

PSALM 98

GENTLE RAIN AND WARM BREEZES

60

Let the rivers clap their hands,
let the mountains sing together for joy.
PSALM 98:8

"Sometimes when I am desperate to see a dramatic display of your power, Lord, I neglect to notice the quiet reminders you place all around me. In the spring, as I watch the earth awaken from its deep winter sleep, I see what extraordinary things you can do with such ordinary things as gentle rain and warm breezes. May I learn to hear your quiet voice, Lord, so you don't have to speak to me in thunder. May I learn to see your power in the everyday order and beauty of the universe, so I don't waste my life waiting for you to prove yourself in a few dramatic exceptions. Thank you that even the earth sings your praise. May I not become so preoccupied with this life that I fail to hear the melodies of heaven. Tune my heart to sing of your grace, Lord, so I can be part of the glorious symphony of praise that the whole universe will one day perform."

¹The LORD reigns, let the nations tremble;
   he sits enthroned between the cherubim, let the earth
         shake.
²Great is the LORD in Zion;
   he is exalted over all the nations.
³Let them praise your great and awesome name—
   he is holy.
⁴The King is mighty, he loves justice—
   you have established equity; in Jacob you have done
         what is just and right.
⁵Exalt the LORD our God
   and worship at his footstool;
   he is holy.
⁶Moses and Aaron were among his priests,
   Samuel was among those who called on his name;
they called on the LORD
   and he answered them.
⁷He spoke to them from the pillar of cloud;
   they kept his statutes and the decrees he gave them.
⁸LORD our God, you answered them;
   you were to Israel a forgiving God,
   though you punished their misdeeds.
⁹Exalt the LORD our God
   and worship at his holy mountain,
   for the LORD our God is holy.

PSALM 99

SAFETY AND OUR GOD

61

The LORD reigns,
let the nations tremble.
PSALM 99:1

"When we live in a nation that can afford the most bombs, it is easy to assume that we can live in safety. And when we can afford to live in the best neighborhoods, it is easy to assume that we can protect ourselves. But our bombs are no match for the powers you can unleash, Lord. And our 'safe' neighborhoods are no shield against the destructive forces of sin. What we need is not better ways of protecting ourselves from evil but more confidence that you are working for our good. May we be known for having the most faith, not the most power. May we be known for having the biggest God, not the biggest bank account. May we be known for the way we bless you, Lord, not just for the way you bless us."

¹Praise the LORD, my soul.
LORD my God, you are very great;
 you are clothed with splendor and majesty.

³He makes the clouds his chariot
 and rides on the wings of the wind.

¹²The birds of the sky nest by the waters;
 they sing among the branches.
¹³He waters the mountains from his upper chambers;
 the land is satisfied by the fruit of his work.

³¹May the glory of the LORD endure forever;
 may the Lord rejoice in his works—
³²he who looks at the earth, and it trembles,
 who touches the mountains, and they smoke.
³³I will sing to the Lord all my life;
 I will sing praise to my God as long as I live.
³⁴May my meditation be pleasing to him,
 as I rejoice in the LORD.
³⁵But may sinners vanish from the earth
 and the wicked be no more.

PSALM 104:1, 3, 12–13, 31–35

SPRINGTIME AND SEASONS

62

The birds of the sky nest by the waters;
they sing among the branches.
PSALM 104:12

"If I could stop the clock in May, I would do it, Lord, for the sights and sounds of your creation coming to life fill my soul with joy and wonder. Thank you for birds that awaken me with singing, for lilacs that intoxicate me with their fragrance, and for flowers that announce the season with such a stunning combination of colors. Thank you that I can see your goodness in the beauty of the earth, hear your words of love whispered in the wind, and feel your heartbeat in the rhythm of the rain. And yes, Lord, thank you for the changing seasons. For although the ecstasy of spring soon will end, even in that there is hope. For in the fleeting moments of 'good times' I am assured that 'bad times' also will end. Thank you for letting us see you in so many glorious displays. Please accept our praise today for all your wonderful ways."

¹Praise the LORD.
Give thanks to the LORD, for he is good;
  his love endures forever.
²Who can proclaim the mighty acts of the LORD
  or fully declare his praise?
³Blessed are those who act justly,
  who always do what is right.

⁷When our ancestors were in Egypt,
  they gave no thought to your miracles;
they did not remember your many kindnesses,
  and they rebelled by the sea, the Red Sea.
⁸Yet he saved them for his name's sake,
  to make his mighty power known.

⁴⁷Save us, LORD our God,
  and gather us from the nations,
that we may give thanks to your holy name
  and glory in your praise.
⁴⁸Praise be to the LORD, the God of Israel,
  from everlasting to everlasting.
Let all the people say, "Amen!"
  Praise the LORD.

PSALM 106:1–3, 7–8, 47–48

THE MIDDLE

63

Blessed are those who act justly,
who always do what is right.
PSALM 106:3

"Like this Psalm, Lord, life begins and ends with easy, exuberant praise. In the beginning, we praise you because we look forward to everything you promise to do. In the end, we praise you because we look back on all the wonderful things you have done. But the middle is another story. The middle is characterized by change and uncertainty, and it is filled with doubt, disappointment, and failure. The middle is difficult because our strength is failing, and we can't yet see the promised land. It is dangerous because we start making bad choices when we begin doubting your ability to accomplish good things. In trying to write our own happy ending, we miss your perfect plan. Many of us are in the middle right now, suspended in uncertainty, hoping for the best yet fearing the worst. Keep us from making foolish choices at this dangerous, difficult intersection. May we turn toward faith, not doubt, and believe the good we can't yet see. Thank you, Lord, for assigning us a role in your unfolding story of redemption. May we praise you even in these middle times, for praise is the script of your divine story, our foretaste of glory, and the only fitting response to the blessed assurance that Jesus is mine."

[1] My heart, O God, is steadfast;
    I will sing and make music with all my soul.
[2] Awake, harp and lyre!
    I will awaken the dawn.
[3] I will praise you, LORD, among the nations;
    I will sing of you among the peoples.
[4] For great is your love, higher than the heavens;
    your faithfulness reaches to the skies.
[5] Be exalted, O God, above the heavens;
    let your glory be over all the earth.

PSALM 108:1–5

WHY?

I will praise you, LORD,
among the nations;
I will sing of you among the peoples.
PSALM 108:3

"Why? Three simple letters; one huge question. Why do you allow evil people to have so much power, Lord? Why do you allow good people to go through so much suffering? Why is my desire for sin so much stronger than my desire for holiness? Why would I rather trust my own instincts than your truth? Why do I believe that self-indulgence, not self-discipline is the way to gain satisfaction? Why is it so much work to rest in you? Surely you have a purpose for our struggles that we cannot comprehend. At the very least they reveal to us how far creation has fallen from your original plan and purpose. May I acknowledge the truth of my condition and proclaim my greatest need—to be close to you."

[1]Praise the LORD.
I will extol the LORD with all my heart
   in the council of the upright and in the assembly.
[2]Great are the works of the LORD;
   they are pondered by all who delight in them.

[7]The works of his hands are faithful and just;
   all his precepts are trustworthy.
[8]They are established for ever and ever,
   enacted in faithfulness and uprightness.
[9]He provided redemption for his people;
   he ordained his covenant forever—
   holy and awesome is his name.

[10]The fear of the LORD is the beginning of wisdom;
   all who follow his precepts have good understanding.
To him belongs eternal praise.

PSALM 111:1–2, 7–10

[1]Praise the LORD.
Blessed are those who fear the LORD,
   who find great delight in his commands.
[2]Their children will be mighty in the land;
   the generation of the upright will be blessed.

PSALM 112:1–2

A Wandering Mind 65

The fear of the LORD is
the beginning of wisdom;
all who follow his precepts
have good understanding.
PSALM 111:10

"I'm ashamed to admit this, Lord, but I am more careful about keeping my dog from wandering than I am my mind. How foolish. For just as surely as a dog follows its nose, my mind follows my emotions and my body follows my mind. And just as surely as a dog smelling its way to adventure finds trouble along the way, so do I. May I not let my mind wander from the truth about your justice to thoughts about injustices done to me, lest I rationalize doing injustice to others. May I not fail to meditate on the truth of your faithfulness, lest I justify my own unfaithfulness. And may I not let my mind wander from the truth about your love, lest I rationalize hatred for anyone who doesn't love me. Thank you, Lord, that when I am lost in a maze of emotion, you are my guide; that when I feel as if I am coming apart, you make me whole; and that when I feel as if everyone is against me, you are the Lover of my soul. Hallelujah, what a Savior!"

¹I love the Lord, for he heard my voice;
 he heard my cry for mercy.
²Because he turned his ear to me,
 I will call on him as long as I live.

⁵The Lord is gracious and righteous;
 our God is full of compassion.
⁶The Lord protects the unwary;
 when I was brought low, he saved me.

¹²What shall I return to the Lord
 for all his goodness to me?
¹³I will lift up the cup of salvation
 and call on the name of the Lord.
¹⁴I will fulfill my vows to the Lord
 in the presence of all his people.

¹⁷I will sacrifice a thank offering to you
 and call on the name of the Lord.
¹⁸I will fulfill my vows to the Lord
 in the presence of all his people,
¹⁹in the courts of the house of the Lord—
 in your midst, Jerusalem.
Praise the Lord.

PSALM 116:1–2, 5–6, 12–14, 17–19

CHURCH THOUGHTS

66

*I will sacrifice a thank offering to you
and call on the name of the LORD.*
PSALM 116:17

"Sometimes I go to church with the attitude that I am doing you a favor by showing up, Lord. Sometimes I sit in my pew waiting for something I dislike so I can go away unmoved, unrepentant, unchanged. Sometimes I show up only to find out how you can improve my life. Forgive me, Father, for making my body get up and attend church while allowing my heart and mind to stay asleep. Forgive me for taking your mercy without giving you my love. May I not allow myself to grow fat and weak by consuming all your blessings for my own enjoyment and pleasure, but instead help me to grow strong by turning all your blessings into words and acts of unselfish praise."

¹Give thanks to the LORD, for he is good;
   his love endures forever.

¹⁰All the nations surrounded me,
   but in the name of the LORD I cut them down.
¹²They swarmed around me like bees,
   but they were consumed as quickly as burning thorns;
   in the name of the LORD I cut them down.

¹⁴The LORD is my strength and my defense;
   he has become my salvation.
¹⁵Shouts of joy and victory resound in the tents of the
      righteous:
   "The LORD's right hand has done mighty things!
¹⁶The LORD's right hand is lifted high;
   the LORD's right hand has done mighty things!"

²⁴The LORD has done it this very day;
   let us rejoice today and be glad.

PSALM 118:1, 10, 12, 14–16, 24

Make the Worst Day Good

67

This is the day the LORD has made;
we will rejoice and be glad in it.
PSALM 118:24 (NKJV)

"I'm sure mosquitoes have their place in creation, Lord, but couldn't you have allowed them to accomplish their task without making life so miserable? That's how I feel about suffering too. I know it has its place, but couldn't you accomplish the job some other way? I admit, though, that the mosquitoes accomplished something good today: in chasing me out of my own backyard, they reminded me how quick I am to abandon spiritual territory whenever I am annoyed or irritated. Discomfort causes me to doubt your goodness, power, and love. But 'good times' lull me into a false sense of spiritual well-being. In good times I can behave pretty well, but in suffering my true spiritual condition is revealed. Thank you, Lord, that even in the worst of times—with the shadow of the cross looming in front of you—you were able to sing this psalm: 'This is the day the Lord has made, we will rejoice and be glad in it.' Thank you, Lord, that every day belongs to you and that praise and adoration can make even the worst day good."

¹I lift up my eyes to the mountains—
  where does my help come from?
²My help comes from the LORD,
  the Maker of heaven and earth.
³He will not let your foot slip—
  he who watches over you will not slumber;
⁴indeed, he who watches over Israel
  will neither slumber nor sleep.
⁵The LORD watches over you—
  the LORD is your shade at your right hand;
⁶the sun will not harm you by day,
  nor the moon by night.
⁷The LORD will keep you from all harm—
  he will watch over your life;
⁸the LORD will watch over your coming and going
  both now and forevermore.

PSALM 121

I Lift Up My Eyes to You 68

I lift up my eyes to the mountains—
where does my help come from?
My help comes from the LORD,
the Maker of heaven and earth.
PSALM 121:1–2

"The pull of earthly concerns weighs me down, Lord. I take on responsibilities you never meant me to have and then complain because I don't have time to get everything done. I buy things I don't need and then grumble because taking care of them is so much work. I give my attention to whomever is making the most noise and then feel guilty because I'm neglecting the people who are most important. Forgive me, Father, for my foolish efforts to find purpose in positions, possessions, and people. I know that you alone are the source of my strength and the guardian of my ways. Even when I am too weary to raise my voice and too tired to lift a finger, I am never too weak to lift my eyes to you. And when I do, I again remember what I so often forget: that the direction I am looking is the way I will go. Help me to keep my eyes focused on Jesus so the enticements and entanglements of the world will lose their power to lure me away from my heavenly purpose."

¹I rejoiced with those who said to me,
   "Let us go to the house of the LORD."
²Our feet are standing in your gates, Jerusalem.
³Jerusalem is built like a city that is closely compacted
      together.
⁴That is where the tribes go up—the tribes of the
      LORD—
   to praise the name of the Lord
   according to the statute given to Israel.
⁵There stand the thrones for judgment,
   the thrones of the house of David.
⁶Pray for the peace of Jerusalem:
   "May those who love you be secure.
⁷May there be peace within your walls
   and security within your citadels."
⁸For the sake of my family and friends,
   I will say, "Peace be within you."
⁹For the sake of the house of the LORD our God,
   I will seek your prosperity.

PSALM 122

ONLY ONE PRINCE OF PEACE

69

Pray for the peace of Jerusalem:
"May those who love you be secure."
PSALM 122:6

"How foolish I am, Lord, to pray for peace when I am unwilling to walk in the ways of your Son, the Prince of Peace. How arrogant I am to expect mercy for myself when I am unwilling to uphold justice for others. How silly I am to settle for what the world wants to sell me when I could have what you want to give me. The world entices me with information, but only you can give me truth. The world offers knowledge, but only you can give me wisdom. The world promises security by forcing people to conform, but only you can give me peace by allowing me to be transformed. This is why I praise you, Lord. This is why I make music to your name. This is why I proclaim your love and sing of your faithfulness."

¹Praise the LORD.
Praise the name of the LORD;
   praise him, you servants of the LORD,
²you who minister in the house of the LORD,
   in the courts of the house of our God.
³Praise the LORD, for the LORD is good;
   sing praise to his name, for that is pleasant.

⁵I know that the LORD is great,
   that our LORD is greater than all gods.

⁸He struck down the firstborn of Egypt,
   the firstborn of people and animals.
⁹He sent his signs and wonders into your midst, Egypt,
   against Pharaoh and all his servants.

¹³Your name, LORD, endures forever,
   your renown, LORD, through all generations.
¹⁴For the LORD will vindicate his people
   and have compassion on his servants.

PSALM 135:1–3, 5, 8–9, 13–14

Change My Hatred to Love

70

I know that the LORD is great,
that our LORD is greater than all gods.
PSALM 135:5

"I know, Lord, that you did not come to make me strong enough to carry the weight of my sin; you came to carry it for me. Forgive me for not releasing it to you. Forgive me for hiding under the comfort of my guilt when you want me to thrive in the warmth of your mercy and the light of your love. Forgive me for thinking that your sacrifice is good enough to get me into heaven but powerless to make me a better person on this earth. I know, Lord, that I am supposed to remember the good you do for me, but I find it much easier to remember the harm others do to me. Please change my hatred into love, my contempt into compassion, and my unreasonable expectations into unselfish acts of mercy. Help me not to be empty-handed when it is my turn to kneel at your throne and place crowns at your feet."

⁸Let the LORD judge the peoples.
  Vindicate me, LORD, according to my righteousness,
  according to my integrity, O Most High.
⁹Bring to an end the violence of the wicked
  and make the righteous secure—
you, the righteous God
  who probes minds and hearts.
¹⁰My shield is God Most High,
  who saves the upright in heart.
¹¹God is a righteous judge,
  a God who displays his wrath every day.
¹²If he does not relent,
  he will sharpen his sword;
  he will bend and string his bow.
¹³He has prepared his deadly weapons;
  he makes ready his flaming arrows.

¹⁷I will give thanks to the LORD because of his
    righteousness;
  I will sing the praises of the name of the LORD
    Most High.

PSALM 7:8–13, 17

WHY DO I DOUBT YOU?

71

*I will give thanks to the LORD because
of his righteousness; I will sing the praises
of the name of the LORD Most High.*
PSALM 7:17

"Why is it, Lord, that I am more afraid of doing your will than not doing it? Where did I get the idea that if I do what you want me to do I'll never get what I want to have? Why do I doubt that what you want for me is good? Is it because belief is more difficult for me than disbelief? You've given me a body that can perceive the world, experience emotion, and draw conclusions, but I use it as if its only purpose is to enable me to enjoy life on earth rather than to prepare me to enjoy life in heaven. I have a hard time not believing what I see, not trusting what I feel, and not relying on what I think. Help me, Lord, to "just believe" that what I can't yet see is more real than what I do see; that what I don't yet feel is better than anything I have ever felt; and that what I haven't yet gained cannot compare to the goodness you want to give. I come to you with my thoughts and feelings and desires in a tangled mess. It's not much, but it's all I have. Please accept my humble worship and make me into someone who exalts your holy name."

¹LORD, our Lord,
how majestic is your name in all the earth!
You have set your glory
in the heavens.
²Through the praise of children and infants
you have established a stronghold against your
enemies,
to silence the foe and the avenger.
³When I consider your heavens,
the work of your fingers,
the moon and the stars,
which you have set in place,
⁴what is mankind that you are mindful of them,
human beings that you care for them?
⁵You have made them a little lower than the angels
and crowned them with glory and honor.
⁶You made them rulers over the works of your hands;
you put everything under their feet:
⁷all flocks and herds,
and the animals of the wild,
⁸the birds in the sky,
and the fish in the sea,
all that swim the paths of the seas.
⁹LORD, our Lord,
how majestic is your name in all the earth!

PSALM 8

POLISHING MY OWN IMAGE 72

When I consider your heavens, the work
of your fingers, the moon and the stars,
which you have set in place, what is mankind
that you are mindful of them, human beings
that you care for them?
PSALM 8:3–4

"O, Lord, my Lord, how quickly I begin to believe that
my name is more important than yours. How easily I
am convinced that I should vindicate myself rather than
worshiping you. How soon your glory fades when I start
polishing my own image. Forgive me for trying to crown
myself with glory and honor. May I learn the simple
praise of an infant and live in the perfect peace of a child
seated in the lap of a loving father. Today as I consider
the awesome wonder of your creation, may I rest in your
greatness, not grow restless or weary from trying to create my own."

² The LORD is my rock, my fortress and my deliverer;
    my God is my rock, in whom I take refuge,
    my shield and the horn of my salvation, my
        stronghold.

⁶ In my distress I called to the LORD;
    I cried to my God for help.
From his temple he heard my voice;
    my cry came before him, into his ears.

¹⁶ He reached down from on high and took hold of me;
    he drew me out of deep waters.

³¹ For who is God besides the LORD?
    And who is the Rock except our God?
³² It is God who arms me with strength
    and keeps my way secure.

PSALM 18:2, 6, 16, 31–32

⁴ Yet their voice goes out into all the earth,
    their words to the ends of the world.
In the heavens God has pitched a tent for the sun.

PSALM 19:4

THE ENEMY OF
SELF-RIGHTEOUSNESS

73

In my distress I called to the LORD;
I cried to my God for help.
From his temple he heard my voice;
my cry came before him, into his ears.
PSALM 18:6

"O, Lord, my Rock and my Redeemer, what more do I need? You give me firm footing in truth, and you clear away the stones strewn along the way that cause me to stumble. You save me from my enemies even when I am my own worst enemy. So often I take your truth and chisel away the parts that make me feel guilty, but then I am left with boulder-size chunks that block the way to you rather than pave it. So I chip away some more, and I end up with a pile of stones that are just the right size for hurling at people. Forgive me, Father, for using your Word to hurt rather than to heal. May I recognize that your real enemy is the self-righteousness in my own heart, not the unrighteousness in anyone else. Unrighteousness you can cure, but self-righteousness, if left unchecked, can be terminal. May I realize that only in admitting my guilt, not denying it, can I get rid of it. I call on you today to save me from enemies—both within and without—and I praise you because you alone have the power to overcome death and sin."

^{25}To the faithful you show yourself faithful,
   to the blameless you show yourself blameless,
^{26}to the pure you show yourself pure,
   but to the devious you show yourself shrewd.
^{27}You save the humble
   but bring low those whose eyes are haughty.

PSALM 18:25–27

^{7}The law of the LORD is perfect, refreshing the soul.
   The statutes of the LORD are trustworthy, making
      wise the simple.
^{8}The precepts of the LORD are right, giving joy to the heart.
   The commands of the LORD are radiant, giving light
      to the eyes.
^{9}The fear of the LORD is pure, enduring forever.
   The decrees of the LORD are firm, and all of them are
      righteous.
^{10}They are more precious than gold, than much pure gold;
   they are sweeter than honey, than honey from the
      honeycomb.
^{11}By them your servant is warned;
   in keeping them there is great reward.
^{12}But who can discern their own errors?
   Forgive my hidden faults.
^{13}Keep your servant also from willful sins;
   may they not rule over me.
Then I will be blameless,
   innocent of great transgression.

PSALM 19:7–13

GUILT IN ITS PROPER PLACE

74

Who can discern their own errors?
Forgive my hidden faults. Keep your
servant also from willful sins;
may they not rule over me.
Then I will be blameless,
innocent of great transgression.
PSALM 19:12–13

"Sometimes I don't like what I see when I look for you, Lord. But maybe that's because I'm looking through lenses still spotted with my own sin. When I can't see your *faithfulness*, perhaps it's because my own faithlessness is in the way. When I can't see your *righteousness*, perhaps it's because I prefer to believe in my own. When I can't see your *love*, perhaps it's because I refuse to look past my own anger. I know I only look for what I want to find, so when I want an excuse for my sin I look for someone else to blame. But if I want forgiveness from my sin, I will look for my personal guilt. May I see my own guilt and put it in its proper place—not in someone else's lap but on the cross of love where Jesus died. Then I will be blameless. Then I will see you as you are. Then I will have reason to sing praises to your name."

[1]You, God, are my God,
    earnestly I seek you;
I thirst for you,
    my whole being longs for you,
    in a dry and parched land where there is no water.
[2]I have seen you in the sanctuary
    and beheld your power and your glory.
[3]Because your love is better than life,
    my lips will glorify you.
[4]I will praise you as long as I live,
    and in your name I will lift up my hands.
[5]I will be fully satisfied as with the richest of foods;
    with singing lips my mouth will praise you.

PSALM 63:1–5

[9]You care for the land and water it;
    you enrich it abundantly.
The streams of God are filled with water
    to provide the people with grain,
    for so you have ordained it.

[12]The grasslands of the wilderness overflow;
    the hills are clothed with gladness.
[13]The meadows are covered with flocks
    and the valleys are mantled with grain;
    they shout for joy and sing.

PSALM 65:9, 12–13

"Be Mine!"

75

You, God, are my God,
earnestly I seek you.
PSALM 63:1

" 'God, you are my God.' I need to let those words sink in when I say them and when I sing them, for they are no ordinary words. They create a perfect valentine—the expression of a heart filled with joy. Sometimes, Lord, we give away a little candy heart that says 'Be Mine,' and we may get one back that says, 'I'm yours.' In effect, you say the words—but they aren't just words: they are a promise from you. Over and over you preface your work with the words, 'So you will know.' Thank you, Lord, that you want your people to know that they belong to you, not to wonder or wish or hope. And not only do we belong to you but you also belong to us. Who can even imagine such a thing! When I consider everything you have given me at no cost, I am ashamed to admit how much I long for things that are costly but have no value. May my life overflow with kindness and generosity as the truth of your love transforms my heart and mind. Thank you, Lord, for letting me call you 'mine.' "

¹May God be gracious to us and bless us
and make his face shine on us—
²so that your ways may be known on earth,
your salvation among all nations.
³May the peoples praise you, God;
may all the peoples praise you.
⁴May the nations be glad and sing for joy,
for you rule the peoples with equity
and guide the nations of the earth.
⁵May the peoples praise you, God;
may all the peoples praise you.
⁶The land yields its harvest;
God, our God, blesses us.
⁷May God bless us still,
so that all the ends of the earth will fear him.

PSALM 67

³²Sing to God, you kingdoms of the earth,
sing praise to the Lord,
³³to him who rides across the highest heavens,
the ancient heavens,
who thunders with mighty voice.
³⁴Proclaim the power of God,
whose majesty is over Israel,
whose power is in the heavens.
³⁵You, God, are awesome in your sanctuary;
the God of Israel gives power and strength to his people.
Praise be to God!

PSALM 68:32–35

THE BRIGHTNESS
OF GOD'S GLORY

76

Proclaim the power of God,
whose majesty is over Israel,
whose power is in the heavens.
PSALM 68:34

"I have learned, Lord, to paste a smile over my face to
mask the confusion, anger, and hurt in my heart. I even
go so far as to consider myself godly for not allowing my
feelings to show. But that's not what Moses did. After
being in your presence, he didn't have to put on a happy
face to cover the darkness of his soul; he had to put on
a veil to shield others from the brightness of your glory
radiating from his face. That is what I too long for, Lord.
I want the world to recognize you when they see me.
Yes, it was indeed a wonder that Moses got to enter your
presence, but today I can celebrate something even more
wonderful—that your presence has entered me, that the
immortal God makes his home in my mortal body, that
the invisible God is being made visible in me. Praise be
to God!"

¹Endow the king with your justice, O God,
　　the royal son with your righteousness.
²May he judge your people in righteousness,
　　your afflicted ones with justice.

¹⁵Long may he live!
　　May gold from Sheba be given him.
May people ever pray for him
　　and bless him all day long.

¹⁷May his name endure forever;
　　may it continue as long as the sun.
Then all nations will be blessed through him,
　　and they will call him blessed.
¹⁸Praise be to the Lord God, the God of Israel,
　　who alone does marvelous deeds.
¹⁹Praise be to his glorious name forever;
　　may the whole earth be filled with his glory.
Amen and Amen.

PSALM 72:1–2, 15, 17–19

THE NEWS VS. THE GOOD NEWS

Praise be to his glorious name forever;
may the whole earth be filled with his glory.
PSALM 72:19

"Sometimes I watch too much news and end up in despair at the amount of evil in the world, Lord. Sometimes when I see what is going on, I wonder why they even call it 'news.' Bad news hasn't been 'new' since the Garden of Eden; good news is the only real news now—and the only really good news is that you are setting this fallen world right. Hallelujah! Sign me up to help! Use me to bless the earth with your goodness by making sure people know about the true good news—the gospel of Jesus Christ. Let's speed the day when once again the whole earth will be filled with your glory."

¹Whoever dwells in the shelter of the Most High
   will rest in the shadow of the Almighty.
²I will say of the LORD, "He is my refuge and my
      fortress,
   my God, in whom I trust."

PSALM 91:1–2

¹It is good to praise the LORD
   and make music to your name, O Most High,
²proclaiming your love in the morning
   and your faithfulness at night,
³to the music of the ten-stringed lyre
   and the melody of the harp.
⁴For you make me glad by your deeds, LORD;
   I sing for joy at what your hands have done.
⁵How great are your works, LORD,
   how profound your thoughts!

PSALM 92:1–5

Tears for Jerusalem

78

Whoever dwells in the shelter
of the Most High
will rest in the shadow
of the Almighty.
PSALM 91:1

"From atop the Mount of Olives, bathed in the light of the sun, your holy city is lovely, Lord, so lovely that it brings tears to my eyes. But your tears for Jerusalem were not for its beauty—they were for its waywardness. While gazing on its glory, you saw its imminent destruction. While riding into the city you listened to the accompaniment of joyful praise on what we call Palm Sunday, but you knew you would leave to the sound of angry curses. I am just as fickle as the crowds that waved branches to welcome you that day. I love following you when you amaze people by doing what seems impossible, but I slink away when I think you might expect me to amaze people by doing something difficult. I like to think I would have followed you all the way to the cross, but I have my doubts. After all, if I don't dare cheer for you at church among people who claim to be on your team, what makes me think I would do so if I were alone in a crowd of your opponents? If I am too much of a coward to shout for joy about history that is certain, how will I ever find the courage to open my mouth about a future that is yet to be written?"

¹It is good to praise the LORD
　　and make music to your name, O Most High,
²proclaiming your love in the morning
　　and your faithfulness at night,
³to the music of the ten-stringed lyre
　　and the melody of the harp.
⁴For you make me glad by your deeds, LORD;
　　I sing for joy at what your hands have done.
⁵How great are your works, LORD,
　　how profound your thoughts!
⁶Senseless people do not know,
　　fools do not understand,
⁷that though the wicked spring up like grass
　　and all evildoers flourish,
　　they will be destroyed forever.
⁸But you, LORD, are forever exalted.

PSALM 92:1–8

MY GUILT

79

For you make me glad
by your deeds, LORD;
I sing for joy at what your hands have done.
How great are your works, LORD,
how profound your thoughts!
PSALM 92:4–5

"Forgive me, Lord, for wasting so much time and energy on trying to absolve myself of guilt. I am learning—finally—that it is more work to find someone to blame for my trouble than to simply take responsibility for it myself. Even in the rare instances when I've been successful in finding someone who is at fault, I've been unsuccessful at getting that person to take responsibility. Big surprise! Why would anyone else want to assume my guilt any more than I do? But here is the great news—you did just that on the cross! I no longer have to search for a place to unload my sin; you've lifted it from my shoulders. You've accomplished the work I could never do for myself. Your work is indeed great, Lord. It is even too wonderful for words. So I turn my praise into a song, and I sing for joy at the work of your hands, for it is your work that enables me to rest from mine."

¹Come, let us sing for joy to the LORD;
  let us shout aloud to the Rock of our salvation.
²Let us come before him with thanksgiving
  and extol him with music and song.
³For the LORD is the great God,
  the great King above all gods.
⁴In his hand are the depths of the earth,
  and the mountain peaks belong to him.
⁵The sea is his, for he made it,
  and his hands formed the dry land.
⁶Come, let us bow down in worship,
  let us kneel before the LORD our Maker;
⁷for he is our God
  and we are the people of his pasture,
  the flock under his care.

PSALM 95:1–7

You Never Run Out of Springtime

In his hand are the depths of the earth,
and the mountain peaks belong to him.
PSALM 95:4

"Thank you, Lord, that you never run out of springtime. Year after year it comes to us through no effort of our own. Thank you that you never get weary of directing the migration of the birds; that you never forget to awaken the trees after a long winter of rest; and that no energy crisis has ever kept you from raising flowers from the cold, dark dirt. Since you do all of this so generously and so faithfully for things that don't resist your promptings, perhaps the only reason you don't do it more often for me is my stubborn determination to do it for myself. Thank you for allowing us to see signs in nature, Scripture, and circumstances that assure us that you are not asleep on the job, that you are indeed at work while the earth is at rest, and that you are at work even when we are restless. Thank you."

¹Sing to the LORD a new song,
  for he has done marvelous things;
his right hand and his holy arm
  have worked salvation for him.
²The LORD has made his salvation known
  and revealed his righteousness to the nations.
³He has remembered his love
  and his faithfulness to Israel;
all the ends of the earth have seen
  the salvation of our God.
⁴Shout for joy to the LORD, all the earth,
  burst into jubilant song with music;
⁵make music to the LORD with the harp,
  with the harp and the sound of singing,
⁶with trumpets and the blast of the ram's horn—
  shout for joy before the LORD, the King.
⁷Let the sea resound, and everything in it,
  the world, and all who live in it.
⁸Let the rivers clap their hands,
  let the mountains sing together for joy;
⁹let them sing before the LORD,
  for he comes to judge the earth.
He will judge the world in righteousness
  and the peoples with equity.

PSALM 98

OUR GOD REIGNS

81

Sing to the LORD a new song,
for he has done marvelous things;
his right hand and his holy arm
have worked salvation for him.
PSALM 98:1

"Thank you, Lord, that all creation awakens from its slumber when you whisper, 'Good morning.' Thank you for spring and its gentle wake-up call—for so many springs that revive us with sweet smells, warm breezes, and stunning beauty. May we see in this repeating drama your attempt to awaken us from spiritual slumber. May it help prepare us for the day when you will announce your arrival with the blast of a trumpet, not the silence of a sunrise—when you will come to rule, not to serve, to judge, not to save. Open our ears to the rhythms of the universe so we can join the rivers in clapping. Open our eyes to the glories of the seasons so we can join the mountains in singing. May we join all creation in proclaiming to the world the good news that 'Our God Reigns.' "

¹I lift up my eyes to you,
   to you who sit enthroned in heaven.
²As the eyes of slaves look to the hand of their master,
   as the eyes of a female slave look to the hand of her
         mistress,
so our eyes look to the LORD our God,
   till he shows us his mercy.
³Have mercy on us, LORD, have mercy on us,
   for we have endured no end of contempt.
⁴We have endured no end
   of ridicule from the arrogant,
   of contempt from the proud.

PSALM 123

⁸Our help is in the name of the LORD,
   the Maker of heaven and earth.

PSALM 124:8

THE PRAYER OF MY LIFE

82

As the eyes of slaves look
to the hand of their master,
as the eyes of a female slave look
to the hand of her mistress,
so our eyes look to the LORD our God,
till he shows us his mercy.
PSALM 123:2

"The songs we sing, Lord, can draw us closer to you—like 'Come, Thou Font of Every Blessing.' *'Prone to wander.'* *That's the story of my life, Lord,* because I keep looking every direction but up. When life is going smoothly, I focus on myself and wander into pride. When life is in turmoil, I focus on others and fall into despair. *'Indebted to grace.'* *That's the song of my life, Lord,* because all of my goodness buys nothing more than a little public approval, which is one of the enemy's most effective seductions. It makes me believe that I have your approval. *'Bind my wandering heart to you.'* *That's the prayer of my life, Lord,* for when I focus on anything other than your goodness, I am in danger of falling into all kinds of evil. Thank you that I don't have to establish a good name for myself by hiding my shame. Instead, as I 'tune my heart to sing thy grace,' I can bear your name and never be ashamed."

¹LORD, remember David
  and all his self-denial.
²He swore an oath to the LORD,
  he made a vow to the Mighty One of Jacob:
³"I will not enter my house
  or go to my bed,
⁴I will allow no sleep to my eyes
  or slumber to my eyelids,
⁵till I find a place for the LORD,
  a dwelling for the Mighty One of Jacob."
⁶We heard it in Ephrathah,
  we came upon it in the fields of Jaar:
⁷"Let us go to his dwelling place,
  let us worship at his footstool, saying,
⁸'Arise, LORD, and come to your resting place,
  you and the ark of your might.
⁹May your priests be clothed with your righteousness;
  may your faithful people sing for joy.'"

PSALM 132:1–9

THE GOOD "NEW" DAYS

83

May your priests be clothed
with your righteousness;
may your faithful people sing for joy.
PSALM 132:9

"How often I forget, Lord, that joy and righteousness are a package deal. I cannot have joy if I am unwilling to be righteous. But I keep trying. I hear so much about 'unconditional love' that I expect your promises to be unconditional as well. I expect to live according to my own rules yet get results that come only from following yours. When I was hot and sweaty this week, I didn't expect you to bring Lake Michigan to my backyard; I went to one of its beaches in Grand Haven instead. Why, then, when I am spiritually dry, do I expect you to refresh me even when I refuse to go where you say I can find living water? May I not miss the joy found only in faithfulness, the satisfaction found only in discipline, or the freedom found only in obedience. May I not miss the opportunity to create 'good new days' because I'm so busy trying to recreate the 'good old days.' Thank you, Lord, for showing us the way to live so we might have joy. Thank you for revealing the meaning of life so we might have purpose. Thank you that we have reason to sing 'Joy to the World' all year long when the ruler of heaven and earth has His rightful place in our hearts."

¹Give thanks to the LORD, for he is good.
His love endures forever.
²Give thanks to the God of gods.
His love endures forever.
³Give thanks to the Lord of lords:
His love endures forever.
⁴to him who alone does great wonders,
His love endures forever.
⁵who by his understanding made the heavens,
His love endures forever.
⁶who spread out the earth upon the waters,
His love endures forever.

²³He remembered us in our low estate
His love endures forever.
²⁴and freed us from our enemies.
His love endures forever.
²⁵He gives food to every creature.
His love endures forever.
²⁶Give thanks to the God of heaven.
His love endures forever.

PSALM 136:1–6, 23–26

Reclaim My Mind

84

Give thanks to the Lord of lords:
His love endures forever.
To him who alone does great wonders,
His love endures forever.
PSALM 136:3

"Perhaps the reason I get so stressed out about my life and the world is because sometimes it seems that your enemy is more visible and vocal than you are, Lord. When I focus on how Satan has turned your beautiful creation into a war zone of hatred, selfishness, and greed, I become angry, selfish, and greedy myself. I want to reclaim what I see you losing. I want to restore order to this chaotic planet. But I'm learning that my ideas about how to do this differ from yours. Reclaim my mind, so I will agree with you about what is good. Restore your image in me, so I will reflect your love, not my anger, to the world. Grant me the faith to believe that your grace is more powerful than my sword. Remind me that my true enemy is the prince of the power of darkness—not those he has deceived. May I realize that my only real strength is in proclaiming the power of your name. To you alone be the glory."

³Great is the LORD and most worthy of praise;
   his greatness no one can fathom.
⁴One generation commends your works to another;
   they tell of your mighty acts.
⁵They speak of the glorious splendor of your majesty—
   and I will meditate on your wonderful works.
⁶They tell of the power of your awesome works—
   and I will proclaim your great deeds.

¹²so that all people may know of your mighty acts
   and the glorious splendor of your kingdom.

¹⁸The LORD is near to all who call on him,
   to all who call on him in truth.
¹⁹He fulfills the desires of those who fear him;
   he hears their cry and saves them.

PSALM 145:3–6, 12, 18–19

THE BEAUTY AND SPLENDOR OF CREATION

85

I will meditate on your wonderful works.
They tell of the power of your awesome works—
and I will proclaim your great deeds.
PSALM 145:5–6

"Whenever we read about the return of astronauts from space, we are reminded of what happens when our bodies are temporarily 'freed' from the natural law of gravity: they become weak. Dear Lord, may that be a reminder to me of what happens to my soul when I insist on being 'free' of spiritual laws: it will be too weak to survive in your kingdom. Today the sky reminds us that your greatness is beyond anything we can fathom. Thank you for natural laws that protect us. Thank you that we don't have to worry about always hanging on to earth so we don't float up toward the sun. Thank you that we don't have to build engines to keep the earth spinning. Thank you for doing all the important things for us so we can do a minimum of work yet have plenty of time left to enjoy the beauty and splendor of your creation. Thank you for the spiritual law that assures us true victory is not physical survival in a world of hate but spiritual surrender to the law of love."

⁷³ Your hands made me and formed me;
   give me understanding to learn your commands.
⁷⁴ May those who fear you rejoice when they see me,
   for I have put my hope in your word.
⁷⁵ I know, LORD, that your laws are righteous,
   and that in faithfulness you have afflicted me.
⁷⁶ May your unfailing love be my comfort,
   according to your promise to your servant.
⁷⁷ Let your compassion come to me that I may live,
   for your law is my delight.

PSALM 119:73–77

MIGHTY ACTS OF NATURE

86

Your hands made me and formed me;
give me understanding to learn your commands.
PSALM 119:73

"When I stop to think about creation, Lord, I am amazed by how much you do with so little. Who could imagine that by combining two invisible, intangible elements you could create something that can nourish all of creation and also generate enough power to illuminate the whole world? But that's what we have in water—something so common that we take it for granted, something so ordinary that we add things to it to make it more exciting. Sometimes that's how I think of your Word, Lord. I know it's good for me, but I wish it had more fizz. I know it's powerful, but I prefer power I can control. Surely you've noticed how upset we get when human energy systems fail. Does it bother you that we pay no attention to the fact that yours never do? We spend lots of money getting water from one place to another, but we barely notice when, with one huge rainstorm, you can move billions of gallons from the Gulf of Mexico to Philadelphia. Forgive us, Lord, for being unmoved by your mighty acts in nature. Forgive us also for refusing to let you move in us. You have shown us the awesome work you can do by combining hydrogen and oxygen. I can't even imagine what you could accomplish if we would let you combine in us the spiritual forces of your wisdom, power, and love. But I know it would be awesome!"

¹Have mercy on me, O God,
  according to your unfailing love;
according to your great compassion
  blot out my transgressions.
²Wash away all my iniquity
  and cleanse me from my sin.
³For I know my transgressions,
  and my sin is always before me.
⁴Against you, you only, have I sinned
  and done what is evil in your sight;
so you are right in your verdict
  and justified when you judge.

¹⁰Create in me a pure heart, O God,
  and renew a steadfast spirit within me.
¹¹Do not cast me from your presence
  or take your Holy Spirit from me.
¹²Restore to me the joy of your salvation
  and grant me a willing spirit, to sustain me.
¹³Then I will teach transgressors your ways,
  so that sinners will turn back to you.

¹⁷My sacrifice, O God, is a broken spirit;
  a broken and contrite heart
  you, God, will not despise.

PSALM 51:1–4, 10–13, 17

THE SOIL OF MY LIFE

87

Create in me a pure heart, O God,
and renew a steadfast spirit within me.
PSALM 51:10

"O, Lord, how tempting it is to believe there is such a thing as a 'victimless' sin. I want to let my mind wander and assume my body won't follow. I want to have my own way without being responsible for interfering with yours. I want to believe that it is only your holiness, not mine, that matters. But I know that is not true because I know how quickly I follow other people into sin and how often I blame other people's failures for my own. I want the soil of my life to be truly holy, Lord, and I want the seeds planted there to be wholly true. May the vices Satan is trying to plant wither and die in the presence of the virtues you are trying to prune. Make me holy, Lord, even as you are holy."

¹Clap your hands, all you nations;
  shout to God with cries of joy.
²For the LORD Most High is awesome,
  the great King over all the earth.
³He subdued nations under us,
  peoples under our feet.
⁴He chose our inheritance for us,
  the pride of Jacob, whom he loved.
⁵God has ascended amid shouts of joy,
  the LORD amid the sounding of trumpets.
⁶Sing praises to God, sing praises;
  sing praises to our King, sing praises.
⁷For God is the King of all the earth;
  sing to him a psalm of praise.
⁸God reigns over the nations;
  God is seated on his holy throne.
⁹The nobles of the nations assemble
  as the people of the God of Abraham,
for the kings of the earth belong to God;
  he is greatly exalted.

PSALM 47

No Shortcuts

God reigns over the nations;
God is seated on his holy throne.
PSALM 47:8

"Many earthly 'kings' are trying hard to bring peace to the small place on earth that bears your name, Lord, but all their attempts and deadlines result only in more fear, more anger, and more violence. It is hard to understand why you allow the misery to continue. Perhaps it's because where you dwell, time is not measured by months of conflict or years of suffering. It is measured by what is being accomplished in human hearts. Thank you, Lord, that your timing is perfect. You came to earth at exactly the right time as Savior, you will come again at exactly the right time as King, and you are taking exactly the right amount of time to prepare us to be good citizens of your eternal kingdom. Even though we would like you to speed the process, we know that when we see the result we will be grateful that you took no shortcuts. We know that waiting on you is not 'doing nothing,' for in waiting we are being perfected. And we know that praising you is not wasting time, for in lifting praise to your name we are preparing for eternity."

^{10}Do not trust in extortion
   or put vain hope in stolen goods;
though your riches increase,
   do not set your heart on them.
^{11}One thing God has spoken,
   two things I have heard:
"Power belongs to you, God,
   ^{12}and with you, Lord, is unfailing love";
and, "You reward everyone
   according to what they have done."

PSALM 62:10–12

EARTHLY RICHES

89

Though your riches increase,
do not set your heart on them.
PSALM 62:10

"Thank you, Lord, for warning us of the danger of earthly riches. Like the Israelites of old who gave all their gold to make a god they could touch, I too am prone to worship what is tangible. I too try to create with my hands what I cannot see with my eyes. I too want to build something people can see to prove the existence of the unseen. In our eagerness to build something great for you, Lord, keep us from thinking that our success is more important to you than our honesty. May we avoid situations that require us to cover up the truth about our financial affairs to remain in good standing with creditors—all the while confession is needed to remain in good standing with you. May we stop thinking of our wealth as proof of how much you love us and see it instead as a test of how much we love you. May we trust you even with financial failure rather than settle for worldly success that would make us guilty of idolatry. May we believe that your strength is made perfect in weakness and that it applies to us, not just to others."

¹I cried out to God for help;
  I cried out to God to hear me.

⁷"Will the Lord reject forever?
  Will he never show his favor again?
⁸Has his unfailing love vanished forever?
  Has his promise failed for all time?
⁹Has God forgotten to be merciful?
  Has he in anger withheld his compassion?"
¹⁰Then I thought, "To this I will appeal:
  the years when the Most High stretched out
      his right hand.
¹¹I will remember the deeds of the LORD;
  yes, I will remember your miracles of long ago.
¹²I will consider all your works
  and meditate on all your mighty deeds."
¹³Your ways, God, are holy.
  What god is as great as our God?
¹⁴You are the God who performs miracles;
  you display your power among the peoples.

PSALM 77:1, 7–14

THE POWER OF HOLINESS

90

Your ways, God, are holy.
What god is as great as our God?
PSALM 77:13

"Holiness: to be set apart from evil; to be used for good. The idea of being set apart is not a popular idea these days, Lord. Like the Israelites, we get jealous of our neighbors who ridicule goodness yet get ahead in business. Like Elijah, we get depressed because we feel as if we are alone in doing good. And so, like the psalmist, we take time to remember that were it not for holiness—your willingness to be set apart for us—we could not live in your presence. The fire of your holiness is both the flame that consumes evil and the energy that empowers goodness. So when we become weary in doing good things, Lord, may we remember the energizing power of your holiness, which was and is and evermore will be."

²When I was in distress, I sought the Lord;
  at night I stretched out untiring hands,
  and I would not be comforted.

⁹"Has God forgotten to be merciful?
  Has he in anger withheld his compassion?"
¹⁰Then I thought, "To this I will appeal:
  the years when the Most High stretched out
      his right hand.
¹¹I will remember the deeds of the LORD;
  yes, I will remember your miracles of long ago.
¹²I will consider all your works
  and meditate on all your mighty deeds."
¹³Your ways, God, are holy.
  What god is as great as our God?
¹⁴You are the God who performs miracles;
  you display your power among the peoples.

PSALM 77:2, 9–14

THE IMPERFECTIONS
OF OTHERS

91

You are the God who performs miracles;
you display your power among the peoples.
PSALM 77:14

"No matter how hard I try or cry or pray, I can't change anyone else's thoughts, desires, or behavior. I'm old enough to know this, Lord, and I've failed often enough to prove it, but I still keep trying to do it. I want others to remain in their discomfort so I can be comfortable. I want others to do what feels unnatural to them so I can have what feels natural to me. I want children to sit down and fold their hands in church, and I want adults to stand up and raise their arms. I should know by now the dangers of false forms of religion that make me feel spiritual but don't change minds or hearts. I should know by now the foolishness of thinking that I can have the ecstasy of resurrection without the agony of crucifixion. Today I surrender to you my desire for perfection in others so you can work on perfecting me. May I use the power of praise to lift up your name in such a way that it will change me into a person worthy of wearing it."

¹⁻³ It seemed like a dream, too good to be true,
    when GOD returned Zion's exiles.
We laughed, we sang,
    we couldn't believe our good fortune.
We were the talk of the nations—
    "GOD was wonderful to them!"
GOD was wonderful to us;
    we are one happy people.
⁴⁻⁶ And now, GOD, do it again—
    bring rains to our drought-stricken lives
So those who planted their crops in despair
    will shout hurrahs at the harvest,
So those who went off with heavy hearts
    will come home laughing, with armloads of blessing.

PSALM 126 (MSG)

Does It Bother You, Lord? 92

Bring rains to our drought-stricken lives.
PSALM 126:4 (MSG)

"Does it bother you, Lord, when we chop down trees so we can grow grass? I suppose this sounds trivial, but when I stop to think about it, I start to wonder if there's a spiritual parallel that should concern us. So let me ask it another way. Does it bother you that we are so quick to get rid of something with roots so we can replace it with something that is essentially rootless? Does it bother you that when it comes to matters of faith we would rather have something soft that tickles our feet than something strong that protects us from the heat? Forgive us for carelessly chopping down the things you provide to protect us—your commands, our marriage covenants, our churches—so we can get a few more things that please us. Keep us from destroying what we will need in the future just so we can have a little more of what we want right now. May we leave the next generation a heritage of true blessing—faith with roots that reach deep for nourishment and with branches that reach out to give shade—not a field of grass that dries up and dies during extended periods of sunshine."

¹Those who trust in the LORD are like Mount Zion,
   which cannot be shaken but endures forever.
²As the mountains surround Jerusalem,
   so the LORD surrounds his people
   both now and forevermore.
³The scepter of the wicked will not remain
   over the land allotted to the righteous,
for then the righteous might use
   their hands to do evil.
⁴LORD, do good to those who are good,
   to those who are upright in heart.
⁵But those who turn to crooked ways
   the LORD will banish with the evildoers.
Peace be on Israel.

PSALM 125

Transform My Thinking

93

Those who trust in the LORD
are like Mount Zion,
which cannot be shaken
but endures forever.

PSALM 125:1

"Once again, Lord, I am guilty of taking credit for what you have done. I look at all the good things I have, and I applaud myself for hard work and smart choices. But even worse, I look at what I don't have and blame you. When I can't afford what I want to buy, I conclude that you are stingy. When I feel unloved, I assume that you are withholding something good from me. And when people and circumstances are beyond my control, I blame you for being powerless. Transform my thinking, Lord, so I will learn to accept my guilt and give you my gratitude. *Thank you for all the beauty you have created*. Although it is too high for me to attain, I can enjoy and appreciate it. *Thank you for all the time you give me*. Although there never seems to be enough to accomplish all my own purposes, I know there is all I need to accomplish yours. *Thank you for all the truth you've revealed*. Although it is more than I can know or hold, I know it is more than enough to uphold me. May the yearnings I cannot satisfy lift me up—not pull me down. May they lead me to heaven—not tie me to earth. May they enable me to please you—not enslave me in futile attempts to please myself."

¹My people, hear my teaching;
    listen to the words of my mouth.
²I will open my mouth with a parable;
    I will utter hidden things, things from of old—
³things we have heard and known,
    things our ancestors have told us.
⁴We will not hide them from their descendants;
    we will tell the next generation
the praiseworthy deeds of the LORD,
    his power, and the wonders he has done.
⁵He decreed statutes for Jacob
    and established the law in Israel,
which he commanded our ancestors
    to teach their children,
⁶so the next generation would know them,
    even the children yet to be born,
    and they in turn would tell their children.
⁷Then they would put their trust in God
    and would not forget his deeds
    but would keep his commands.

PSALM 78:1–7

AMAZE OTHERS

94

We will tell the next generation
the praiseworthy deeds of the LORD,
his power, and the wonders he has done.
PSALM 78:4

"Thank you, Lord, that your goodness is meant to be seen and heard by all. Thank you for physical senses with which we can perceive your glory in the beauty of the universe, and thank you for spiritual gifts and talents with which we can magnify and amplify what we see and hear for those who are still spiritually blind and deaf. Many are still tuned to the droning of Satan's voice and cannot hear you, but they can hear us praise you. Many are still blinded by the artificial lights of the world and cannot see your glory, but they can see us worship you. May our lives of praise and worship amaze people with the excellent use of our spiritual gifts. May we never apologize for giving our best. May we never ridicule those who want to glorify you through excellence. May we never be ashamed of doing things well. The church is never healthier than when all believers are reaching their full potential and using their gifts in effective, amazing, and remarkable ways for your glory."

¹How lovely is your dwelling place,
    Lᴏʀᴅ Almighty!

³Even the sparrow has found a home,
    and the swallow a nest for herself,
where she may have her young—
    a place near your altar,
    Lᴏʀᴅ Almighty, my King and my God.

⁴Blessed are those who dwell in your house;
    they are ever praising you.

¹⁰Better is one day in your courts
    than a thousand elsewhere;
I would rather be a doorkeeper in the house of my God
    than dwell in the tents of the wicked.
¹¹For the Lᴏʀᴅ God is a sun and shield;
    the Lᴏʀᴅ bestows favor and honor;
no good thing does he withhold
    from those whose walk is blameless.
¹²Lᴏʀᴅ Almighty,
    blessed is the one who trusts in you.

PSALM 84:1, 3, 4, 10–12

What Comes from Your Hand?

95

I would rather be a doorkeeper in the house of my God
than dwell in the tents of the wicked. For the LORD God
is a sun and shield; the LORD bestows favor and honor.
PSALM 84:10–11

"Sometimes the only honest prayer I can offer is this: 'I want to want your will, Lord. I want to want what you desire.' Is that anything you can work with? It won't be easy, because I keep jumping ahead or falling behind. I keep trying to see where you're taking me before trusting you to get me there. When I am in the shadow, I assume that I am under a thundercloud rather than in the shelter of your wings. When I am in the sunlight, I worry that it's not going to last. When the wind starts to howl, I hold on so it can't blow me away rather than let go so it can lift me up. I need to take a lesson from the birds, who follow your rhythm and always know when it's time to fly or rest, who don't try to repeat yesterday or change tomorrow. Right now, this minute, open my hands to release the past and relinquish the future. May I accept what comes from your hand each day as a carefully chosen gift. If it's wind, may I catch it and soar. If it's stillness, may I wait in quiet contentment, knowing that the moving of your Spirit will not leave me stranded but will take me to the next place at your proper time. Thank you that even your name reminds me to live in the 'now,' for you are the present tense, the great 'I AM,' the One who contains all that is and was and is to come. Blessed be your holy name, Lord God Almighty."

¹When the LORD restored the fortunes of Zion,
   we were like those who dreamed.
²Our mouths were filled with laughter,
   our tongues with songs of joy.
Then it was said among the nations,
   "The LORD has done great things for them."
³The LORD has done great things for us,
   and we are filled with joy.
⁴Restore our fortunes, LORD,
   like streams in the Negev.
⁵Those who sow with tears
   will reap with songs of joy.
⁶Those who go out weeping,
   carrying seed to sow,
will return with songs of joy,
   carrying sheaves with them.

PSALM 126

GREEN LAWNS AND TEARS

96

Those who sow with tears
will reap with songs of joy.
PSALM 126:5

"I don't want to be disrespectful, Lord, but my neighbors with automatic sprinkling systems have better-looking lawns than people like me who depend on you for rain. And frankly, I would rather water my flowers myself when I'm outside than to have to come inside because you are doing the job with a downpour. This confession of my impatience and independence should give me a clue as to why I don't particularly care for the idea that tears are required to produce the crop you want to grow. It also gives evidence of my limited vision. For even though a lush, green lawn looks nice, it can't compare to a field of flowers that flourish with no human attention whatsoever. And although I enjoy gazing at my simple pots of petunias or visiting an elaborate arboretum with a grand display of exotic plants, nothing man-made can compare to the grandeur of rivers and forests and snow-topped mountains that humans haven't yet touched. If you can produce all this beauty with a few rainy days, why is it so difficult for me to believe that you can produce a harvest of joy from my few tears? Maybe that's the miracle you want to do. Maybe that's the beauty you want me to see. Maybe that's the faith it takes to make my heart unfold like a flower before you."

¹Hear me, LORD, and answer me,
    for I am poor and needy.
²Guard my life, for I am faithful to you;
    save your servant who trusts in you.
You are my God . . .

⁷When I am in distress, I call to you,
    because you answer me.
⁸Among the gods there is none like you, Lord;
    no deeds can compare with yours.

¹⁰For you are great and do marvelous deeds;
    you alone are God.

¹³For great is your love toward me;
    you have delivered me from the depths,
    from the realm of the dead.
¹⁴Arrogant foes are attacking me, O God;
    ruthless people are trying to kill me—
    they have no regard for you.

¹⁷Give me a sign of your goodness,
    that my enemies may see it and be put to shame,
    for you, LORD, have helped me and comforted me.

PSALM 86:1–2, 7–8, 10, 13–14, 17

Poor and Needy

97

For great is your love toward me;
you have delivered me from the depths,
from the realm of the dead.
PSALM 86:13

"I admit, Lord, that I am poor and needy. One tiny wrinkle in the rug can cause me to fall on my face and become helpless. One small blip in the economy can cause my investments to come crashing down and make all my careful planning useless. One short look in the wrong direction can change the course of my life and send me hurtling toward spiritual destruction. Yes, Lord, I admit that I am poor and needy, but I must also admit how often I try to minimize my neediness in foolish ways. Instead of trusting you to comfort me when I fall, I refuse to get out of my comfortable chair. Instead of trusting you to protect me during times of trouble, I keep trying to fortify my own security system. Instead of believing that you know the way I should go, I keep looking over my shoulder to find an easier route. Help me to learn, loving Father, that a life worth living is found not in being safe but in trusting your protection. Indeed, there is no other god like you, for you not only tell me these things but you also show me these things. Your love didn't just find a way for sinners to be reconciled to you; it led the way. At Calvary you showed a sign of your goodness that puts other gods to shame. At Calvary you suffered the worst affliction so we might receive the best comfort."

¹I will sing of the LORD's great love forever;
    with my mouth I will make your faithfulness known
    through all generations.
²I will declare that your love stands firm forever,
    that you have established your faithfulness in heaven
        itself.

⁵The heavens praise your wonders, LORD,
    your faithfulness too, in the assembly of the holy
        ones.
⁶For who in the skies above can compare with the
    LORD?
    Who is like the LORD among the heavenly beings?
⁷In the council of the holy ones God is greatly feared;
    he is more awesome than all who surround him.
⁸Who is like you, LORD God Almighty?
    You, LORD, are mighty, and your faithfulness
        surrounds you.

¹⁴Righteousness and justice are the foundation of your
        throne;
    love and faithfulness go before you.
¹⁵Blessed are those who have learned to acclaim you,
    who walk in the light of your presence, LORD.

PSALM 89:1–2, 5–8, 14–15

A Pilgrim

98

Blessed are those who have learned
to acclaim you, who walk in the light
of your presence, LORD.
PSALM 89:15

"Thank you, Father, for the assurance that I am involved in something more important than myself, something bigger than my problems, and something higher than my pursuit of pleasure. Sometimes, though, when I can't see what it is, I am tempted to attribute to Satan the work you are doing. Protect me from this dangerous way of thinking. May I never conclude that a particular 'thing' could not possibly be from you simply because I don't understand it or because it is unpleasant. May I learn to acclaim you for your faithfulness, not blame you for my doubt. I do indeed want to walk worthy, Lord. And to do so I know that I need to spend less time as a tourist sauntering along Easy Street and more as a pilgrim heading for High Street. Please order my steps in your Word, dear Lord, and enable me to do your will."

¹² But you, LORD, sit enthroned forever;
    your renown endures through all generations.

¹⁵ The nations will fear the name of the LORD,
    all the kings of the earth will revere your glory.
¹⁶ For the LORD will rebuild Zion
    and appear in his glory.

²¹ So the name of the LORD will be declared in Zion
    and his praise in Jerusalem
²² when the peoples and the kingdoms
    assemble to worship the LORD.

²⁵ In the beginning you laid the foundations of the earth,
    and the heavens are the work of your hands.
²⁶ They will perish, but you remain;
    they will all wear out like a garment.
Like clothing you will change them
    and they will be discarded.
²⁷ But you remain the same,
    and your years will never end.
²⁸ The children of your servants will live in your presence;
    their descendants will be established before you.

                                        PSALM 102:12, 15–16, 21–22, 25–28

¹ Praise the LORD, my soul;
    all my inmost being, praise his holy name.

                                        PSALM 103:1

GLORY, HONOR, AND PRAISE

99

So the name of the LORD will be declared
in Zion and his praise in Jerusalem when the peoples
and the kingdoms assemble to worship the LORD.
PSALM 102:21–22

"I know you don't need any spin doctors, Lord, but sometimes when your name and reputation are under attack I start making excuses for you—as if I'm embarrassed by the way you're handling the universe. This shows how twisted my thinking can be. You do not need me to defend you; you need me to conform to you. And when I am truly concerned about conforming my life to you, I won't need to worry about how you look to the world. For it is not you who needs to be reconciled to the world; it is the world that needs to be reconciled to you. May I not profane your name by using it to sell products to the world. I want to exalt your name by proclaiming that you alone are the Wonderful Counselor, Mighty God, Prince of peace, whose name is worthy of all glory, honor, and praise."

[1] Praise the LORD.
Praise the LORD from the heavens;
   praise him in the heights above.
[2] Praise him, all his angels;
   praise him, all his heavenly hosts.
[3] Praise him, sun and moon;
   praise him, all you shining stars.
[4] Praise him, you highest heavens
   and you waters above the skies.
[5] Let them praise the name of the LORD,
   for at his command they were created,
[6] and he established them for ever and ever—
   he issued a decree that will never pass away.

[13] Let them praise the name of the LORD,
   for his name alone is exalted;
   his splendor is above the earth and the
       heavens.

PSALM 148:1–6, 13

PROCLAIM GOD'S PRAISE

100

Praise the LORD.
Praise the LORD from the heavens;
praise him in the heights above.
PSALM 148:1

" 'Doing what comes unnaturally' pretty much describes the spiritual life, Lord. It is natural to grumble when bad things happen and not to be grateful for all the bad things that don't happen. It's natural to get angry and want revenge but not to be loving and offer forgiveness. It is natural to criticize but not to praise. Yet love and mercy and praise make up the fuel that energizes the spiritual life. Why is this so difficult for me to learn? I need only look at myself. I certainly am more motivated to do good by those who affirm what I do right than by those who only point out what I do wrong. Is this true of you too? Is this why praise is so important? May we put this into practice with one another as well. May we energize each other with legitimate praise rather than paralyze each other with unfair criticism. Give us love for those who betray us, patience with those who criticize us, and compassion for those who are so focused on everything that is wrong that they are unable to enjoy all that is good. May we remember that we are part of creation and that we are closest to perfection when we are using our lips and our lives to proclaim your marvelous praise."

Index of Psalms

A Word about
Julie Ackerman Link

Julie worked in publishing and started her career at Zondervan, where she served as managing editor of devotional and self-help books. Julie began writing articles for *Our Daily Bread* in 2000. During the next fifteen years, her insightful and inspiring articles touched millions of lives around the world. Among the books Julie wrote for Discovery House were *Above All, Love* and *A Heart for God*. After a long battle with cancer, Julie died on April 10, 2015.

Enjoy this book? Help us get the word out!

Share a link to the book or
mention it on social media

Write a review on your blog, on a retailer site,
or on our website (dhp.org)

Pick up another copy to share with someone

Recommend this book for your
church, book club, or small group

Follow Discovery House on
social media and join the discussion

Contact us to share your thoughts:

 @discoveryhouse   @DiscoveryHouse

Discovery House
P.O. Box 3566
Grand Rapids, MI 49501 USA

Phone: 1-800-653-8333
Email: books@dhp.org
Web: dhp.org